Canada

Theo L. Hills
Sarah Jane Hills

Professor Theo L. Hills is a well-known geographer, and chairman of the Education Committee of the Canadian Association of Geographers. He is Associate Professor of Geography at McGill University, in Montreal. Mrs. Hills until recently worked with the Arctic Institute of North America. Both Professor and Mrs. Hills have lived and traveled in Canada for many years. Their studies and travels have helped them to describe the land and people of Canada in an authentic and interesting manner.

EDITORS AND ADVISORS

LIFE IN OTHER LANDS

ALASKA	AUSTRALIA
CANADA	HAWAIIAN ISLANDS
MEXICO	CHINA
BRAZIL	JAPAN
SOUTH AMERICA	INDIA
AFRICA	SOVIET UNION

CANADA

Theo L. Hills

Sarah Jane Hills

THE FIDELER COMPANY — GRAND RAPIDS, MICHIGAN

Grateful acknowledgement is made to the following for permission to use the illustrations found in this book:

Alberta Government—Edmonton: Pages 52, 74, 123, 125, and 127.
Art Gallery of Toronto: Page 116.
British Columbia Government—Victoria: Pages 24, 28, 48, 66, 72, and 153.
Brown Brothers: Page 140.
Canada Department of Agriculture—Ottawa: Pages 39 and 51.
Canada Wide Feature Service—Montreal: Pages 15, 33, 34, 37, 40, 46, 62, 70, and 71.
Canadian Broadcasting Corporation—Toronto: Pages 100, 117, and 129.
Canadian National Railways—Montreal: Pages 9, 103, and 130.
Canadian Pacific Railway Company—Montreal: Pages 47, 61, 82, 91, 104, and 141.
Capital Press Service—Ottawa: Pages 41, 53, 89, 101, 110, 142, and 147.
City Art Gallery—Bristol, England: Page 137.
Dubroy—Deschenes, Quebec: Page 146.
Ford Motor Company of Canada—Toronto: Page 84.
Fur Trade Journal of Canada—Toronto: Pages 42 and 76.
Malak—Ottawa: Pages 27, 63, and 112.
Morant—Banff: Page 96.
National Film Board—Ottawa: Pages 12, 14, 16, 17, 18, 19, 20, 26, 31, 35, 36, 38, 43, 44, 56, 57, 58, 59, 60, 67, 68, 69, 73, 81, 85, 102, 105, 109, 113, 120, 126, 131, 133, 134, 138, 143, 144, 145, 148, 149, and 150.
National Gallery of Canada—Ottawa: Page 114.
Ontario Department of Travel and Publicity—Toronto: Pages 29, 30, 45, 54, 65, 77, 80, 92, 94, 106, 118, 119, 121, 122, 124, 128, 135, and 139.
Rowed—Jasper: Pages 3, 13, 21, 23, 49, 75, 79, and 97.
Shell Oil Company: Page 86.
Taylor—Toronto: Page 111.
Trans-Canada Air Lines—Montreal: Page 99.
Winnipeg Bureau of Travel and Publicity: Pages 87, 88, 107, 108, and 132.

TO THE TEACHER

The editors of this book believe that the secret of successful learning lies in motivating the student to *think*. This fundamental principle has been effectively stated by John Dewey in his book *Democracy and Education:* "The sole path to enduring improvement in the methods of instruction and learning consists in centering upon the conditions which exact, promote, and test thinking. Thinking *is* the method of intelligent learning; of learning that employs and rewards mind." Our great need is to lead students to think purposefully.

Purpose and Interest

Purpose and interest are the most important elements of thinking. To expect students to read and think about geography without first helping them find a purpose, or an interest, is to invite their failure. The first step in teaching geography must be exposing the student to a highly challenging environment that will arouse his natural curiosity. The teacher may create this environment with the help of the proper learning aids. A good filmstrip or large pin-up board pictures will let all the students of the class see vivid views of life in Canada. Good geography pictures are a powerful aid for creating interest and developing purpose on the part of the student. The clear, lighted pictures in a good filmstrip that shows vivid, fascinating views of Canada and its people appeal to every student's natural curiosity. If a Canada filmstrip or a collection of good geography pictures about Canada is not available, the teacher may group the students so that the entire class can share most effectively all of the copies of this textbook that are in the classroom. If the attention of each member of the class is centered on the same picture at the same time, the students may enjoy as a group visual experiences that are almost as satisfactory as those made possible by a filmstrip.

The teacher may judge the quality of the interest created with the aid of these pictures by the number of questions that flow naturally from normal students whose curiosity has been aroused. These questions should be recorded, discussed, and revised by the group. Those that offer a true challenge to the students' efforts open the way for profitable study about Canada.

(A Canada filmstrip designed for use with this book may be secured from Informative Classroom Picture Publishers, Grand Rapids 2, Michigan, for $3.95.)

When a sufficient degree of interest has been aroused, the filmstrip projector is turned off. Successful motivation has brought forth a group of questions for which the class is seeking answers. During this period of study, large thought-provoking pictures displayed on the pin-up board and used by individual students will serve as effective learning aids and source material.

[A portfolio of Canada geography pictures, size 9¼" x 12³⁄₁₆" has been published for use with this book and other geography textbooks. It may be secured from Informative Classroom Picture Publishers, Grand Rapids 2, Michigan. (The Canada portfolio — 48 plates — $3.95.) Fifteen chapters of loose-leaf text are included for reference use by the students.]

Help the Student Understand

In this book pictures, captions, and text are scientifically planned to help the student create in his mind many crystal-clear mental images that are necessary for understanding Canada. The book is complete in itself and easy to comprehend. The average student can use it successfully on his own level with a minimum amount of assistance from the teacher if his interest has been aroused. To help the student build vivid mental images, the editors have included over a hundred photographs that were carefully selected for their value in showing the reader what he might see on a well-planned "geography" trip to Canada. Each picture is accompanied by an informative caption that encourages the student to think and to form meaningful associations.

The pictures and their captions are a great aid for comprehension and for vocabulary building.

Three Levels of Reading Ability

To help the teacher provide for the great differences in the reading ability found in the average class, this book is designed for use on three ability levels. It makes possible purposeful investigation and purposeful reading by students on each of these levels:

1 — A few of the students will read purposefully only the geography pictures, some of the maps, and many of the captions.

2 — Most of the students will read the pictures and the captions, the maps, and much of the text.

3 — Some will read with good comprehension all of the text, the pictures and their captions, and the maps.

In each class there will be a few students who will read the book most effectively on the first level only. Each of these students urgently needs a copy of the book for his individual use. The challenging pictures and captions in each chapter make it possible for these students to share many important learning experiences. The teacher will be pleased to observe the amount of essential information that is gained and the thought-provoking experiences that are shared by these students, even though they are reading at the first level.

In the average geography class in which Canada is studied, nearly every student will be able to use this book successfully. Each will read at one or more of these three levels at various times as the study progresses. But all will make the same trip through Canada, and all students will gain valuable experiences in geography. As a result, all will be able to participate more effectively in group discussion and in group activity, based on an understanding of the important features of the geography of Canada.

Attitudes

Our goal should be one of helping the student acquire an interest in geography that will insure his being alert throughout his life to geographic changes. We should help him acquire a knowledge of how these changes affect him, his country, and the world. If the teacher does not guide, direct, and stimulate the student in such a manner that he acquires this abiding geographic interest, he has failed to reach the desired objective. To develop this attitude requires that the geography class be one in which vivid, challenging learning aids are used in a concrete and interesting manner with the help of a teacher who is vitally interested in the subject.

How Many Copies Are Needed?

Each teacher must answer the question: "How many copies of this textbook are needed for my class?" Each teacher must personally assume responsibility for securing the learning aids that will enable his students to learn successfully. If the teacher believes it is desirable to study Canada carefully so that each member of the class may see the land and understand the people, it is most desirable to have enough copies of the book so that one will be available for each student. However, this book can be used successfully in considerably smaller quantities. If ten copies of this textbook are used in the manner described above and are supplemented by other books, a good Canada filmstrip, and Canada teaching pictures, they can effectively serve a class of thirty children. All of the children in the class will share the deeply rewarding experience of seeing Canada and meeting the people. They will form many of the true-to-life mental images that they would form if they were actually to visit Canada.

The editors invite you to use this book in the manner explained here so that you may observe the quality of the results it is possible for you to achieve with this plan. The plan is based on the laws of learning and on generally accepted principles of education.

The Editors

CONTENTS

CANADA

he Coast Mountains. * Several ranges of steep mountains stretch along Canada's Pacific Coast.

CHAPTER ONE
THE LAND

Canada covers most of the northern half of the continent of North America. It is larger than the whole United States, including the state of Alaska. The northern tip of Canada is less than five hundred miles from the North Pole, and the southern boundary borders the United States. Three oceans sweep Canada's coasts. To the east is the Atlantic and to the west the Pacific. Far to the north is the icy Arctic Ocean.

Let us visit the regions of this vast country shown on the map on page 10. We will travel on one of the transcontinental railroads, following the route shown on this map.

* Please see glossary, page 154.

Canada is a vast land of forests, mountains, deep valleys, fertile lowlands, and wide flat pla

The Pacific Mountain Region. We begin our journey in Vancouver,* a large port city on the Pacific Coast of Canada. From here we travel eastward through the rugged Pacific Mountain Region. (See map above.) For a time, our railroad leads through the fertile valley of the Fraser River. This is only one of many deep valleys that cut through the high mountains in this part of Canada. Through our train window we see the steep slopes of the Coast

10

Canada covers most of the northern half of North Americ
It is bordered by the Atlantic, Pacific, and Arctic
oceans, and by the United States.

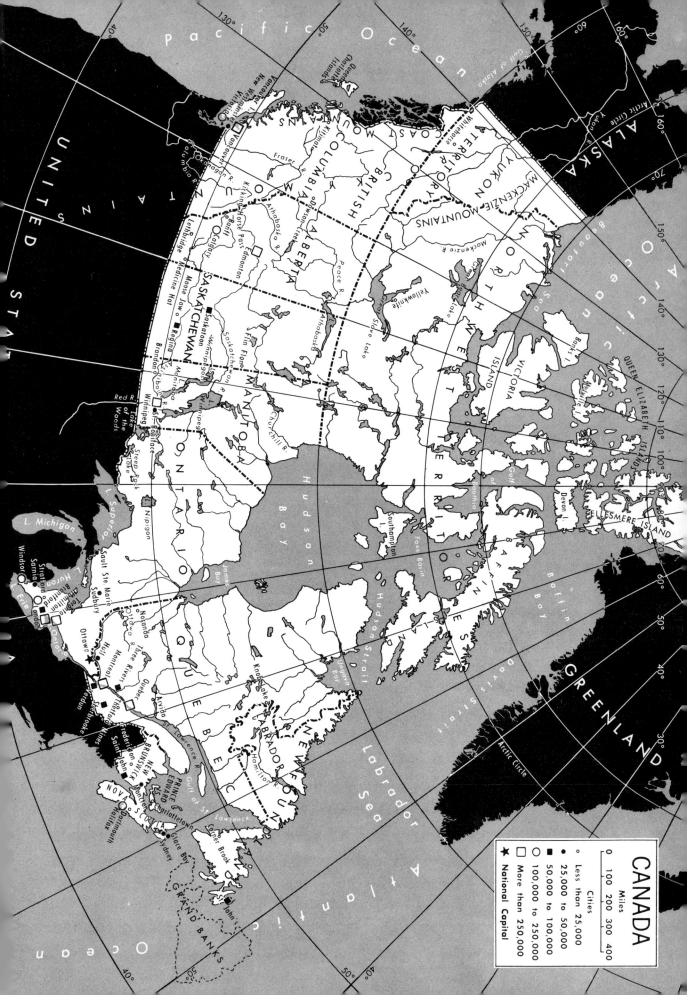

A fertile river valley in the Pacific Mountain Region. This is only one of many deep valleys that cut through the mountains in this part of Canada.

Mountains.* (See map on page 11.) Dense forests of cedar trees, giant Douglas firs, and many other evergreens cover these mountains. Our train moves slowly as we climb through the rugged uplands that lie east of the Coast Mountains. After a journey of many miles, the jagged peaks of the Rocky Mountains loom into sight. Many of these snow-capped peaks rise more than eleven thousand feet into the sky.

This towering wall of mountains forms a barrier to railways and roads. Fortunately, there are several passes through which trains can travel. Even these passes are high above sea level, however. As our train winds through Kicking Horse Pass,* we reach an elevation of 5,339 feet. This is the highest point in our journey.

The belt of mountains through which we are traveling is part of a highland region that extends along the western edge of the entire

he snow-capped Rocky Mountains lie along the eastern border of the Pacific Mountain Region.

continent of North America. As our train winds down the eastern slopes of the Rockies, we leave this rugged region and enter the great Western Plains.

The Western Plains. Canada's Western Plains are part of a vast region of plains and plateaus that stretches through the entire continent of North America. (See map on page 8.) At the western edge of the plains the land is gently rolling. To the east it becomes very flat. (See picture below.) As we ride across this wide, flat plain, we pass some of the richest farmland in the world. It is summer, and a golden blanket of waving wheat covers the countryside as far as we can see. Giant grain elevators stand near the railroad tracks. Here and there, the steel towers of oil wells rise high above the fields. Seldom do we pass a tree.

On the Western Plains are gently rolling grazing lands and some of the world's richest farmland

e Canadian Shield. This rocky region of lakes and forests covers about one half of Canada.

The Canadian Shield. Now our railroad leads through the lonely, rocky countryside of the Canadian Shield. This region occupies almost one half of Canada. (See map on page 10.) Among the valleys and low, rounded hills are thousands of lakes and rivers. Forests cover much of the land. Valuable minerals are dug in the lonely mines of this region. The soil is poor and thin, however, and we pass very few farms.

The Canadian Shield is shaped somewhat like a horseshoe, because Hudson Bay in the center has taken a giant's bite out of the land. (See map on page 10.) Thick ice covers this great bay for many months of the year.

Hudson Bay lies in the center of the Canadian Shield. On the southwest is a lowland region.

Along the southern border of Hudson Bay is a low, almost level plain which is eight hundred miles long. This is called the Hudson Bay Lowland. It is a region of marshlands and forests. Few people live here.

The Arctic Islands. The cold, lonely islands of the Canadian Arctic stretch far to the north of Hudson Bay. Some of them lie within a few hundred miles of the North Pole. No railroads reach into this part of Canada. A Canadian passenger on our train tells us that some of these islands look like rugged mountains jutting out of the sea. During most of the year they are covered with ice and snow. Eskimos are among the very few people who live in this northern region.

The Great Lakes—St. Lawrence Lowlands. As we continue to travel eastward across Canada, we pass along the north shore of the Great Lakes. Soon we enter the most densely populated region of Canada, the Great Lakes—St. Lawrence Lowlands. Almost two thirds of the people of Canada live in this area. Two of Canada's largest cities, Toronto* and Montreal,* are found here.

The western half of these lowlands is almost surrounded by three of the Great Lakes. (See map on page 10.) Rolling lowlands border the lake shores and rise gently to form low hills in the heart of this area. Much of the country we pass through is rich farm and pasture land.

Canada's Arctic Islands. Some of these lonely islands look like mountains jutting out of the sea.

The eastern half of this region lies along the St. Lawrence River. Here the land is flat and fertile. We see long, narrow fields stretching back from the river banks. Often our train passes through busy industrial towns and cities.

The Great Lakes and the St. Lawrence River have been linked together by canals and locks to form the St. Lawrence Seaway.* (See map on page 90.) Ocean liners from many different countries sail along this great water highway.

The Great Lakes—St. Lawrence Lowlands. Most of Canada's people live in this fertile region

The Maritime Region. In the fertile valleys of this part of Canada there are many farms.

The Maritime Region. Let us cross the St. Lawrence River and travel toward Halifax,* Canada's largest port city on the Atlantic Coast. We are riding through the part of Canada known as the Maritime Region. The name Maritime means near the sea. As we can see on the map on page 10, this part of Canada is almost completely surrounded by the ocean. It is a land of old, worn-down

19

mountains, fertile valleys, and rocky coasts. In the valleys are many farms. Little villages huddle along the rocky coasts, and small fishing boats lie anchored in sheltered harbors. When we reach the busy city of Halifax, we end a journey of more than four thousand miles. We have traveled the entire width of the continent of North America.

DO YOU KNOW

1. Locate Canada's geographical regions on the map on page 10. Which region occupies almost half of Canada?
2. What oceans sweep Canada's coasts?
3. Describe the rich farmland of Canada's Western Plains.
4. What does the name Maritime mean? Describe the Maritime Region in Canada.

The Maritime Region of eastern Canada is almost surrounded by the waters of the Atlantic Ocean

In summer, the Arctic Region has twenty or more hours of sunshine each day.

CHAPTER TWO
THE CLIMATE

Canada is a land of changing seasons and many climates. As we travel through this vast country, we will see how the climate differs from place to place. We will also discover the reasons for these differences. Our journey will be made in winter, but we will also learn about the summer climate of each place we visit.

Canada's climate north of the Arctic Circle.* First we board a plane that takes us northward into Canada's Arctic Region. Our plane lands on Baffin Island,* deep within the Arctic Circle. (See map on page 11.) Although it is noon, the sky is nearly dark on this cold January day. Here, on the northern part of Baffin Island,

* Please see glossary, page 154.   21

the sun does not rise above the horizon for two months in winter. The Arctic Region has this long winter night because the northern part of the earth is tipped away from the sun during this season. Therefore, at this time of year the sun's rays cannot reach the lands which lie north of the Arctic Circle.

We are surprised to learn that less snow falls in the Arctic Region than in southeastern Canada. Our guide tells us that there is not enough moisture in the cold, dry, arctic air to make a heavy snowfall possible. However, the snow that falls remains throughout the long, dark winter. Here and there, the snow has been piled into drifts by strong winds.

If we visited the Arctic Region during the short summer season, we would see little ice and snow. Instead, a bright blanket of poppies, buttercups, and other gaily colored flowers would cover the ground in many places. The plains would be green with moss and lichens.*

Long hours of summer sunshine bring this change to the Arctic. In summer, the northern part of the world is tipped toward the sun. Lands lying north of the Arctic Circle receive twenty or more hours of sunlight each day.

The climate of Canada's Pacific Mountain Region. From Baffin Island we fly southwest to Canada's Pacific Mountain Region. Our plane crosses the high Rockies and the forested Coast Mountains.* (See map on page 11.) We notice that in many places the mountain slopes are covered with a deep, white blanket of snow. After a trip of more than two thousand miles, we land at Vancouver,* a large port city on Canada's Pacific Coast. (See map on page 11.)

In Vancouver we find mild, wet weather. There are several reasons why winters are not very cold along Canada's west coast. First, the high mountains we just crossed shelter this coast from icy arctic winds. Second, a warm ocean current called the North Pacific Drift flows past the western coast of Canada. (See map on page 25.) It brings to this coast the mildest winter temperatures in Canada.

It rains much of the time that we are in Vancouver. Westerly winds that sweep in from the Pacific Ocean bring this rain. They are warmed and absorb moisture as they blow across the North Pacific Drift. When these winds reach the Coast Mountains, they are forced to rise sharply. As they rise, they are cooled and lose their moisture in the form of rain or snow. Much of the Pacific Coast receives between sixty and one hundred inches of rainfall each year. Dense forests of tall evergreen trees grow on the rainy slopes of the Coast Mountains.

A white blanket of snow covers many parts of the Pacific Mountain Region during the winter.

In summer, the weather is often clear and pleasantly cool along Canada's Pacific Coast. The waters of the Pacific Ocean become warm much more slowly than the land. Winds blowing across these cool waters bring mild summer days to this part of Canada. However, farther inland in the valleys of the Pacific Mountain Region, summer days are warmer. Cooling breezes from the ocean cannot reach these inland valleys.

The climate of Canada's Western Plains. Now we travel eastward to the great Western Plains. Here we find bitterly cold weather. Winds from the Arctic Region have brought freezing winter temperatures to all of Canada east of the Rockies. Winter days are not always cold on the plains, however. At times, a warm, dry wind called the "chinook" blows in from the west. The chinook sometimes raises the temperature on the plains as much as forty

Summer days along the Pacific Coast are often clear, mild, and pleasantly cool.

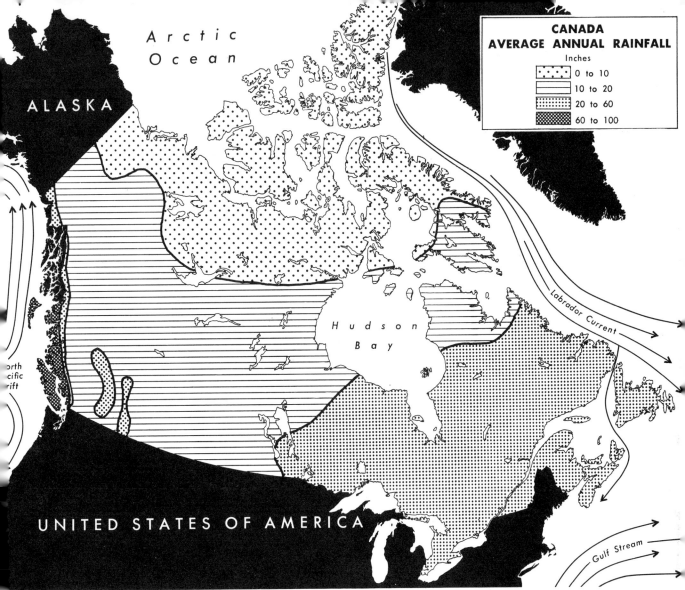

Rainfall is heavy on Canada's Pacific Coast. The air is drier in the arctic and on the plains.

or fifty degrees in a few hours. Then heavy snows melt quickly, exposing the stubble on the grainfields.

If we visited the Western Plains in summer, we would find the weather hot and usually dry. Warm, damp, westerly winds from the Pacific Ocean lose their moisture in the mountains and reach the plains as hot, dry winds. So little rain falls here that there are very few trees. Before white settlers arrived to cultivate the land, grass covered this vast plain. Today most farmers grow wheat and dry-weather crops.

25

Summer on the Western Plains is hot and usually dry. Farmers grow crops that need little moistu

In addition to the dry westerly winds, dry winds from the Great Plains of the United States sometimes blow across Canada's Western Plains in summer. At times they bring heat waves and drought.* During these hot, dusty days, the soil dries up and crops turn brown.

The climate of southeastern Canada. From the plains, we fly to southeastern Canada. In winter, icy winds from the Arctic bring many clear, cold days to this part of the country. Often, however, moisture-filled air from the south meets this cold arctic air, causing very heavy snowstorms. Many of these storms occur in the Great Lakes–St. Lawrence Lowlands. Storms also come to these lowlands from the Atlantic Ocean, the Gulf of Mexico, and the Western Plains.

In summer, hot, moist winds from the Gulf of Mexico sometimes reach southeastern Canada. These winds bring warm summer weather and many thunderstorms to this part of the country. Summer temperatures are not always high in southeastern Canada, however. Sometimes the days are cloudy and cool.

The climate of Canada's Atlantic Coast. We end our journey on the Atlantic Coast. As we fly along the coast of Labrador, we see below us a rocky, treeless shore line. (See map on page 11.) A cold ocean current called the Labrador Current flows southward along this coast. (See map on page 25.) The icy waters of this current bring chilling temperatures to this coastal region.

Farther south, off the coast of the Maritime Region, the icy Labrador Current meets a warm current called the Gulf Stream.* (See map on page 25.) The warm waters of this current bring

Winter in most of Canada is cold and snowy. Winds from the arctic bring freezing temperatures.

milder temperatures to the coasts of the Maritime Region. Here, winter days are not as cold as they are farther inland. Winds blowing over the Gulf Stream absorb moisture and bring much snow and rain to this region.

Summer days along the Atlantic Coast are pleasantly cool and often foggy. These fogs occur when the warm air over the Gulf Stream mingles with the cold air over the Labrador Current.

Summer soon turns into the long, lovely season of fall. Here, as in other parts of Canada, autumn days are crisp and often clear, and the woods are bright with colored leaves.

DO YOU KNOW

1. Explain why a winter night lasts from two to three months in Canada's Arctic Region.
2. On the map on page 25, find areas of Canada receiving 60 inches of rain or more.
3. How does the North Pacific Drift affect the climate of Canada's Pacific Coast?
4. Describe the summer climate in Canada's Western Plains

Canadian apple blossoms. In springtime the many apple orchards in Canada burst into bloom

A Canadian family. Ancestors of about half of Canada's people came from the British Isles.

CHAPTER THREE
THE PEOPLE

Canada is one of the largest countries in the world, yet less than eighteen million people live within its borders. This is only about one tenth as many people as live in the United States. Most of Canada's people live in the southern part of the country. All of the large cities are in this area. This is natural, for here the soil is fertile and the climate warmer than in the rest of Canada.

A Scottish dance. The ancestors of many present-day Canadians came from the British Isles.

About one half of Canada's people are of British descent. The ancestors of nearly half the people in Canada came from England, Ireland, Wales and Scotland. Today, many people of British descent live in all the Canadian provinces except Quebec.* The largest number of British Canadians live in the province of Ontario.*

Let us pay a visit to Toronto,* the capital city of Ontario. (See map on page 11.) As we walk through the main business section of this large city, we notice that many of the people here have light hair and blue eyes. They are dressed like people in other cities in Canada and the United States. Some of the people with whom we speak have strong British accents. They have probably come to Canada from the British Isles since World War II. Most of the products that we see in the shops are also sold in the United States. At a corner, we pass a large United Church. This church is a union of Methodist, Congregational, and Presbyterian churches. Nearly half of the British Canadians are members of the United Church.

Almost one third of Canada's people are of French descent. Now let us travel northeastward to the city of Quebec.* (See map on page 11.) As we walk along the city streets, we notice that many of the people are shorter than those we met in Toronto. They have dark hair and dark eyes, like their French ancestors. The men are wearing business suits. The women and girls are dressed very much

A United Church service. Nearly half of the British Canadians belong to the United Church.

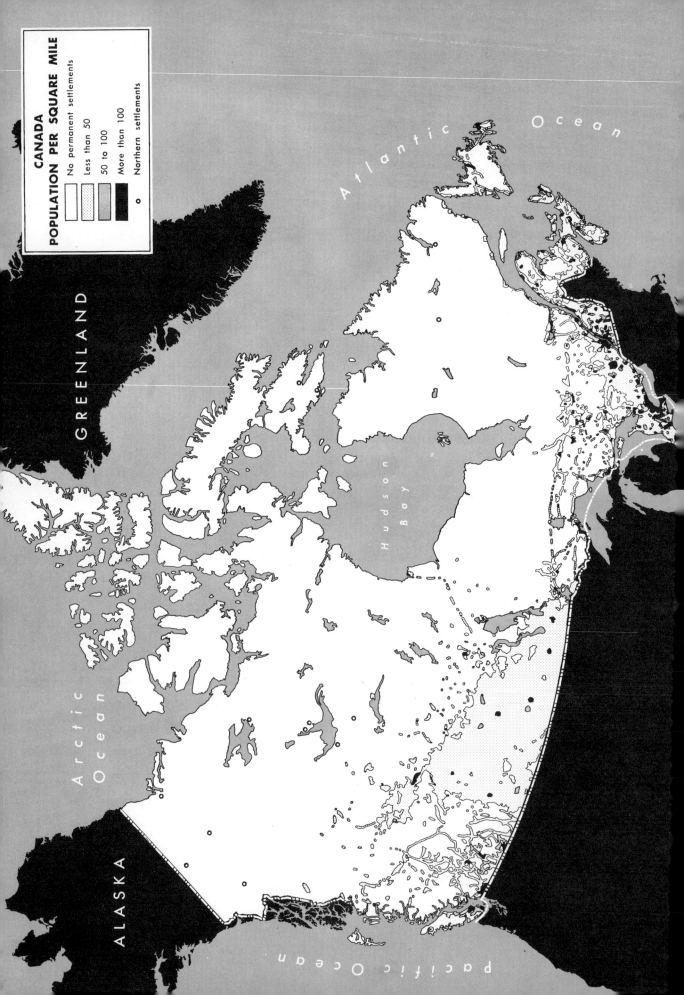

CANADA
POPULATION PER SQUARE MILE

No permanent settlements
Less than 50
50 to 100
More than 100
Northern settlements

Atlantic Ocean

GREENLAND

Hudson Bay

Arctic Ocean

ALASKA

Pacific Ocean

A maple-sugar party in Quebec.* Most of the people of this province are of French descent.

like women and girls in other large cities in Canada and the United States.

As we enter a bookshop, we notice that the sign over the door is printed in French and in English. Inside the shop, we hear people speaking French. The shopkeeper smiles and tells us that most of his books are printed in French. More than nine tenths of the people in the city of Quebec are of French descent. He also tells us that about eight out of ten people who live in the province of Quebec* are French. With pride he says, "The French people were the first white settlers in Canada."

33

*Population. About nine tenths of Canada's people live within two hundred miles of the United States border. All the large cities are in this area.

Sunday dinner in a farm home. Most Canadians enjoy a high standard of living.

A visit with a French farm family. Now we leave the city and drive to one of the prosperous farms that border the St. Lawrence River. (See map on page 11.) All around us the land is green with summer crops. The farm we are going to visit belongs to Monsieur Trudeau. He and his large family live on land that he inherited from his father. Every member of the family helps to plant, harvest, and store crops for the long winter.

We stop in front of the Trudeaus' small, white farmhouse. The steps and window frames of the house are painted pink. The Trudeaus, like other French Canadians, are very fond of bright colors. On some of the floors inside the house there are lovely hooked rugs. Madame Trudeau made these during the winter. In the kitchen we see an electric stove and a refrigerator. There are electric lights in every room. Even the barn has a few electric lights.

The members of the Trudeau family do many things together. In the evenings they sometimes sing the old French songs their ancestors sang long ago. On Sunday mornings they dress in their

High Mass in a Roman Catholic chapel. Most Canadians of French descent are Roman Catholics.

finest clothes and go to the church in a neighboring village. Like other French Canadians, the Trudeaus are Roman Catholics.

Other people of Canada. People from Germany, the Ukraine,* Scandinavia,* the Netherlands, Poland, and other European countries have made their homes in Canada during the past sixty years. Many of these people have come since World War II. They have brought with them their native folk songs, dances, and beautiful handicrafts. These people have become loyal Canadians and are working in many parts of the country.

Ukrainian* Canadians. In recent years, people from many countries have come to Canada.

Farmers attend an evening discussion. About one sixth of Canada's workers are farmers.

The people of Canada earn their living in many different ways. Today, most Canadians enjoy a high standard of living. Almost one fourth of Canada's workers earn their living in mills and factories. About one sixth of the workers are farmers. Some work in trades and professions. Many other Canadians work in the mines, in the forests, and on fishing boats.

---DO YOU KNOW---

1. With the aid of the text, and the map on page 32, tell where most Canadians live.
2. Use pictures in this chapter to help describe different peoples of Canada.
3. What language, beside English, is spoken widely in the province of Quebec?
4. From what countries have many people come to Canada since World War II?

Indians who live on forested reserves* often make their living by cutting trees for wood pulp.

CHAPTER FOUR

INDIANS AND ESKIMOS

Indians and Eskimos have lived in Canada for many thousands of years. We believe that the ancestors of these peoples came to North America from Asia. They probably crossed a narrow strip of water called the Bering Strait,* which lies between the U.S.S.R.* and Alaska. From Alaska, some of the tribes traveled south and east to make their homes in what is now Canada.

Today, fewer than one out of every hundred people in Canada are Eskimos or Indians. There are many more Indians than Eskimos. Most of these Indians live and work on reserves* of land that were set aside for them many years ago by the government.

Some Indians live in cities and towns outside these reserves. Let us travel through Canada and visit some of the Indians and Eskimos.

Indians in the Maritime Region. We begin our trip by visiting the Micmac Indians of the Maritime Region. (See map on page 10.) Before white men came, the Micmacs hunted in the forests and fished in the streams and rivers. Today, hunting and fishing are not the main occupations of these people. They work at many jobs. In the fall, many Micmacs travel from farm to farm harvesting potatoes. Some cross the border into the United States to work on farms in Maine. Others pick blueberries or cut Christmas trees. Many Indians work in fish canneries, and the women often make potato baskets. Farther inland, where most of the reserves are

Indians on the Western Plains once hunted buffalo. Today they grow wheat and raise cattle.

forested, Indians cut trees for wood pulp and lumber. Some work as guides for tourists who come to fish in the streams and lakes.

Indians in the Great Lakes—St. Lawrence Lowlands. We leave the Maritime Region and travel westward to the Great Lakes—St. Lawrence Lowlands. (See map on page 10.) Many of the Iroquois* Indians of this region leave their reserves to work in Montreal factories. The Indians of the Caughnawaga Reserve* near Montreal* are famous as construction workers on great skyscrapers. Many of these people also make their living by farming. They live in modern homes rather than in the bark-covered "long houses"* of several centuries ago.

An Indian family in Quebec.* Like many Indians, the father of this family is a fur trapper.

An Eskimo igloo. Eskimos are among the very few people who live in Canada's Arctic Region.

Now we visit a band of Algonquin* Indians living to the north of the Great Lakes—St. Lawrence Lowlands. These Indians cut trees for lumber and wood pulp from their forested reserve. They trap such animals as mink, beaver, and marten* for their valuable pelts. If we wished to go fishing or hunting, we would probably take an Algonquin as our guide.

Indians of the Canadian Shield. We continue our journey northwest to the forests of the Canadian Shield. (See map on page 10.) The Indians who live here were once great hunters and trappers. Today there are fewer animals to hunt and trap than in earlier years. Therefore, many of these Indians must earn their living by working in forests or in mines. Some help build railroads and radar stations in northern Canada.

41

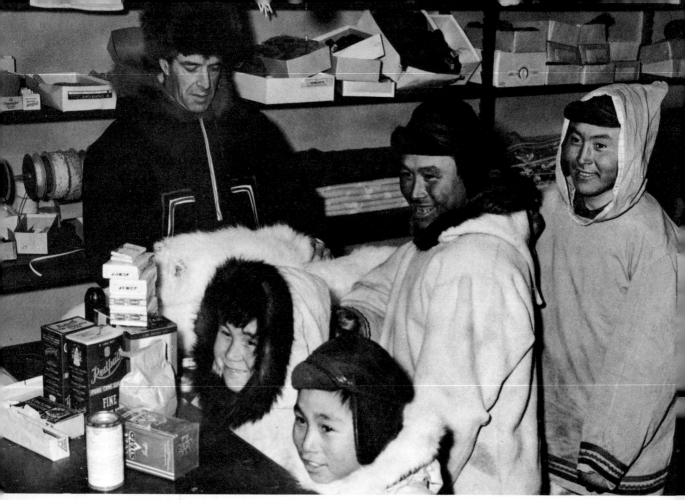

At a trading post. Eskimos trade fox furs and sealskins in return for food and supplies.

Indians of the Western Plains. We now travel to the wide Western Plains. Before white men came to Canada, Indians in this region obtained nearly all their food and clothing from the buffalo which roamed the plains. Today, there are no buffalo for the Indians to hunt. Many now make their living by growing grain and raising cattle. During the harvest season, they often pick sugar beets on farms outside the reserves. Some bands* of Indians have become rich from oil deposits discovered on their reserves.

Indians of the Pacific Mountain Region. Now we are traveling through the rugged Pacific Mountain Region that lies west of the plains. As we drive through the fertile valleys and plateaus of this mountainous area, we pass prosperous cattle ranches and blooming orchards. Some of these are owned by Indians.

42

Our road leads westward to the woodlands along the Pacific Coast. Here we come to another Indian reserve. In this village stand several tall, brightly painted totem* poles. The Indians we see here have always made their living by fishing. Their ancestors were spearing and trapping long before the white men came to Canada. In sturdy, ocean-going canoes made of hollowed-out logs, they hunted whales and seals. Today, many of these Indians earn their living on modern commercial fishing boats.

Eskimos of the Arctic Region. In a plane that has skis instead of wheels, we fly northeastward to Baffin Island.* Here, north of the Arctic Circle,* the sea is frozen over. We must land on the ice. Everywhere the countryside is white with snow, and the wind is icy cold.

Dog sleds pulled by Huskies* are still the chief method of transportation for most Eskimos.

We travel by dog sled to a settlement of four or five igloos. Here we are met by a group of Eskimos. They are short, smiling people with copper-colored skin and dark hair. Their pants and parkas* are made of caribou* skin to protect them from the cold. They ask us to join them for a meal of seal meat and tea.

Many years ago, the Eskimos made their living by hunting seal, caribou, and the few other kinds of animals that live in this bleak land. Today, there are not always enough animals for food. The Eskimos must trade fox furs and sealskins at a trading post in return for food, guns, and other supplies.

On a summer visit to the Canadian Arctic, we travel on a supply ship to Southampton Island.* Our ship brings mail and enough supplies for a year to the tiny settlements along the arctic coasts. The Eskimos are now wearing cotton or wool parkas and pants.

An Eskimo family. In summer, most Eskimos wear cotton or wool parkas* and live in tents.

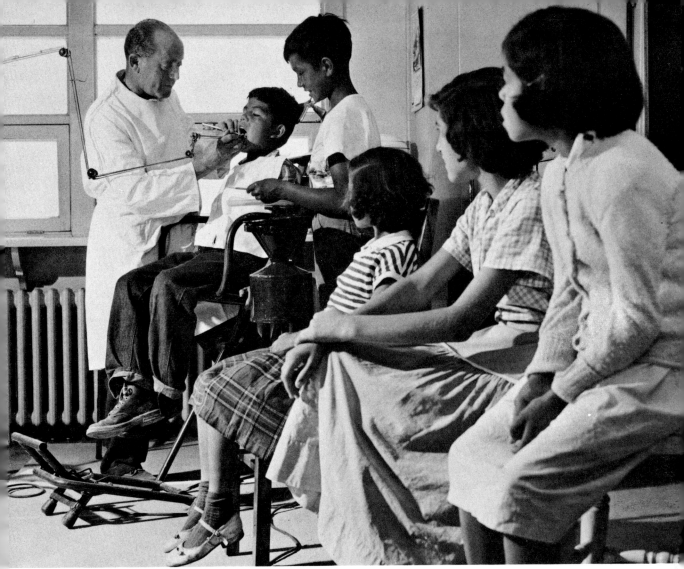

A dental clinic. The Canadian government provides medical care for the Eskimos and Indians.

They are living in tents made of canvas or sealskin. Most of the men are away in their kayaks* or motorboats hunting seal, walrus, and whale.

The Canadian government is helping the Eskimos and Indians. The Canadian government is working hard to improve the health of the Eskimos and Indians. Many of these people are sick with tuberculosis and other diseases. Hospitals and nursing stations have been built to care for them. The health of some Indians is not good because they do not eat the proper foods. They are being taught how to choose and prepare the right kinds of food. Many

Eskimo families also receive powdered milk, baby foods, and other supplies from the government.

The government is helping the Eskimos and Indians learn how to make a better living. There is not always enough game for the Eskimos to make their living by hunting. A few of these people have been sent to southern Canada to learn new trades and skills. Others are being encouraged to make beautiful carvings which can be sold to people in the rest of the world. On most Indian reserves, schools have been established where Indians may obtain the education they need to make a better living.

---DO YOU KNOW---

1. Who were the first peoples to make their home in Canada?
2. Using pictures and the text, tell how Indians and Eskimos make their living.
3. Using pictures in this chapter, describe the clothing of the Eskimos.
4. In what ways is the Canadian government helping the Indians and Eskimos today?

An Eskimo worker. Today, many Eskimos and Indians are learning new ways of making a living

rchards in the Pacific Mountain Region. Many kinds of fruit trees grow in this part of Canada.

CHAPTER FIVE
FARMING AND GRAZING

Canada is one of the world's great food-producing countries. However, when we look at the maps on pages 50 and 55, we see that only a small part of this vast country is used for farming and grazing. Forests and tundras* cover about half the land. Along the west coast lies a wide belt of high mountains and plateaus. Most of the Canadian Shield is too rocky and hilly to be cultivated. In part of northern Canada, the growing season is too short

47

Digging potatoes. In the Pacific Mountain Region, crops are grown in the deep river valleys.

for raising most crops. It is only in the southern part of the country that there are enough warm days for many kinds of crops to grow. Here, also, the most fertile soil is found. For these reasons, most farms and ranches are in southern Canada.

To learn more about farming in Canada, let us visit the main regions of this great country. We will make our trip by train, starting in the belt of mountains that stretch along the western edge of Canada.

The Pacific Mountain Region. As our train twists and turns through the Pacific Mountain Region, we can see that little of this rugged countryside is suitable for growing crops. The only farmland is in deep valleys and on the lower slopes of hillsides. In the Fraser River Valley,* we pass dairy farms and vegetable gardens which produce food for the people of Vancouver.* Traveling on through the beautiful Okanagan Valley,* we see many apple, peach, and pear trees. Orchards also cover the lower slopes of hillsides in other valleys. Mild winters and warm summers make this a good fruitgrowing region.

Now our train winds down the eastern slopes of the Rocky Mountains. In the foothills we pass many ranches where fine beef cattle and sheep are raised.

The Western Plains. We continue to travel eastward across the wide, flat Western Plains. (See map on page 10.) This is Canada's

cattle roundup. There are many cattle ranches on the plains and in the foothills of the Rockies.

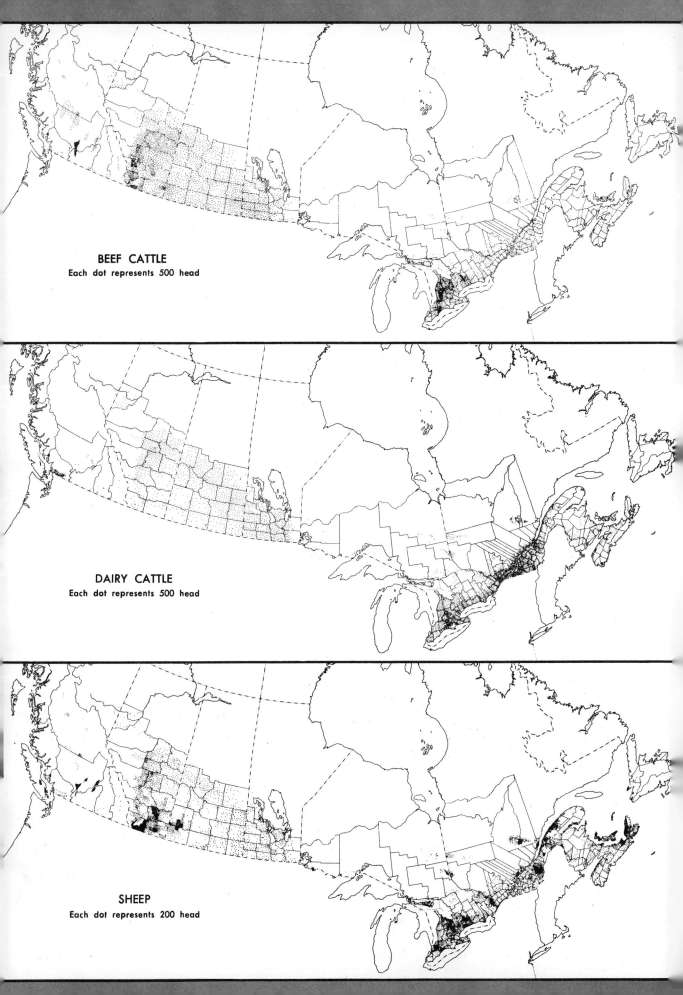

BEEF CATTLE
Each dot represents 500 head

DAIRY CATTLE
Each dot represents 500 head

SHEEP
Each dot represents 200 head

Harvesting spring wheat. Canada exports wheat and flour to many countries of the world.

richest farming region. Here are the deep black soils, the summer rains, and the hot dry harvest season necessary for raising a good wheat crop. In the fall, lines of great combines* move across these vast fields, cutting and threshing the golden wheat. The wheat is then passed into waiting trucks, which carry it to huge storage elevators near the railroad lines. Canada exports wheat and flour to many countries of the world. In addition to wheat, farmers in this region raise oats, barley, flax, sugar beets, and potatoes.

The Canadian Shield. We leave the wide plains and travel eastward through the southern part of the great Canadian Shield. This is a region of thin soils, rocky hills, lakes, and forests. Here, very few people make their living by farming.

The Great Lakes—St. Lawrence Lowlands. Now we are riding through the western half of the Great Lakes—St. Lawrence Lowlands.

Cattle and sheep are raised on the Western Plains,
in the Great Lakes — St. Lawrence Lowlands,
and in parts of the Maritime Region.

Irrigating sugar beets. The richest farmlands in Canada are on the Western Plains.

This is in the southern part of the province of Ontario.* The map on page 10 shows us that this rich farming area is almost completely surrounded by three of the Great Lakes. We also see that it lies farther south than any other part of Canada. Summers here are warm, and the growing season is longer than in most other parts of the country.

The farms we see here are much smaller than those on the plains. We pass neat fields enclosed by wire fences, or by rows of poplar trees. On the hillsides close to the lake shores are apple orchards and vineyards. Mild winds from the lakes bring temperatures warm enough for growing fruit in this region. On other farms we see fields of tobacco, potatoes, vegetables, and other crops. Dairy herds here produce milk and cream for the large number of dairies in this area.

Soon our train enters the eastern half of the Great Lakes—St. Lawrence Lowlands. This is in the southern part of the province of Quebec.* (See map on page 11.) Here we see long, narrow fields stretching back from the banks of the St. Lawrence River. Long ago, there were very few roads in this area and most farmers had to travel by boat. Because the St. Lawrence River was such an important water highway, each farmer wanted to own a section of the river bank. The rest of his farm stretched back from the water's edge like a long, narrow ribbon. Today, the farms are still this shape.

Many dairy cattle are raised in the Great Lakes—St. Lawrence Lowlands of Canada.

As we ride on through southern Quebec, we pass groves of sugar-maple trees as well as fields of crops and pastures. These maple groves are usually called "maple bushes." In the spring, before the snows have melted, farmers tap* the maple trees. Then they attach silver-colored buckets to the trees to collect the sap as it drips out. When the buckets are full, the farmers and their helpers empty them into large cans on horse-drawn sleds. They take the sap to small wooden huts in the bush. There it is boiled in vats over a wood fire until it becomes thick maple syrup. Nine tenths of Canada's maple syrup and maple sugar is produced in this part of Quebec.

A tobacco-curing* shed. Many kinds of crops grow in the Great Lakes—St. Lawrence Lowlands.

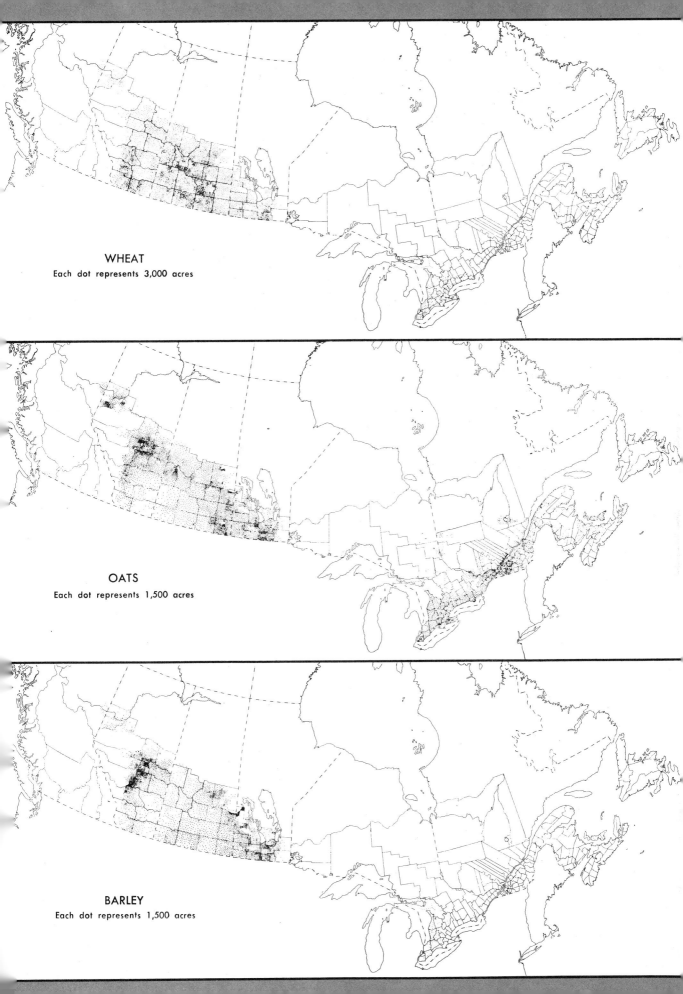

WHEAT
Each dot represents 3,000 acres

OATS
Each dot represents 1,500 acres

BARLEY
Each dot represents 1,500 acres

Collecting sap from sugar-maple trees. Most of Canada's maple sugar comes from southern Quebec

The Maritime Region. Now we enter the Maritime Region. (See map on page 10.) This is a region of great contrasts. In Newfoundland* there are stretches of rocky, barren land. Here crops and grass grow best in valleys and on sunny slopes that are sheltered from icy winds that blow across the Labrador Current.* However, on Prince Edward Island* we find rich, red soil and a milder climate. Potatoes and other crops grow in great quantities here. We also pass good farmland in the many fertile valleys of the Maritime Region. Farmers in the St. John Valley* in New Brunswick* raise oats and hay, which they feed to dairy cows. Large, sweet apples grow in the Annapolis Valley* of Nova Scotia.*

We end our journey on the Atlantic Coast of the Maritime Region. Here we see the small fields of farmers who are also part-time fishermen. It is difficult to make a living by farming here, because the summers are so cool, and in many places the soil is thin and poor.

DO YOU KNOW

1. Explain why only a small part of Canada can be used for farming and grazing.
2. On the maps on pages 50 and 55, locate the chief farming and grazing areas.
3. Describe how syrup is made from the sap of maple trees in southern Quebec.
4. List the farm crops that are shown in pictures in this chapter.

---

farm on Prince Edward Island.* There are many areas of good farmland in the Maritime Region.

Cutting a giant fir tree. Dense, green forests cover much of the land in the Pacific Mountain Regi

CHAPTER SIX

FORESTS

If we could fly high enough in an airplane to view all of Canada at once, we would see that a great blanket of green forests spreads across much of the land. These forests reach from the Atlantic to the Pacific, covering more than a third of Canada. We would not see forests in the extreme north. There the climate is too cold for trees to grow. The map on page 64 shows that Canada's vast forests may be divided into three main regions. Let us visit each of these regions.

The Pacific mountain forest. We are driving northward from the city of Vancouver* to visit a logging camp in the Pacific mountain forest. A breeze, warmed by the ocean, blows inland. The day is mild and humid. On either side of the road are rich, green forests. We see Douglas fir trees two hundred feet high, spruce

Topping* a tree in the Pacific mountain forest. Canada's tallest trees grow in this region.

trees, giant hemlocks, and cedars. Sixty to one hundred inches of rain falls in this region each year, helping these trees to grow tall. They are the tallest in Canada.

As we near the logging camp, we hear the sound of axes and the chugging of an engine. From deep in the forest comes the buzz and whine of power saws. As we enter the camp, we see several long, low buildings. They are constructed of rough boards. The camp will be needed for only a few seasons, so it was built as cheaply as possible.

A crane picks up a heavy log deep within a forest of the Pacific Mountain Region.

A log boom. Logs tied together into rafts called "booms" are pulled by tugboats to the sawmills.

A little way from the camp, we see a steel cable strung high above the ground between tall trees. This cable is called a "sky line." It is about two hundred yards long. As we watch, a carriage travels along the sky line. A long steel rope, which hangs from the carriage, is fastened to the end of a log. The log is being dragged from the forest to a storage yard nearby. We hear the chugging sound of a little steam engine that runs the sky line. Little engines like this are often called "donkey engines." Sky lines and steam engines are commonly used in this area to take logs from the forest to storage yards. From the yards, they are carried by truck or train to the water's edge.

Pulpwood piled in neat rows. Trees of the northern forest are small but hardy.

In the water the logs are tied into rafts or "booms," and pulled by tugboats to sawmills. (See picture on page 61.) There, the rough logs are cut into planks and boards for lumber. More than half of Canada's lumber comes from the Pacific mountain forest.

The northern forest. Canada's northern forest region stretches from Alaska to the shores of the Atlantic. It spreads as far north as the frozen tundras.* The trees of this forest are small but very hardy. Among them are such evergreens as spruce, balsam fir, and jack pine.

Breaking a log jam. Logs are dragged from the forest to the nearest river. From there, they float downstream to the pulp and paper mills.

Trees in this great forest are usually cut in the autumn and winter. The logs are dragged out of the woods on tractor-drawn sledges and piled beside frozen rivers. When the ice melts in the spring, the logs float downstream to the pulp and paper mills. Sometimes the trees are cut in spring or summer. The logs are then carried by truck to the mills.

Pulp and paper mills are found in many parts of Canada. These mills are powered by electricity produced by Canada's many rivers. Beside each mill is an enormous pile of logs cut into short

Canadian forests. Three great forest regions cover more than one third of the land in Canada.

A sawmill. Logs are lifted from the water onto a moving ladder which carries them into the mill.

lengths. In the mills, these logs are ground to pulp. This pulp is then pressed into paper.

The mixed forest. Southeast of the great northern forest lies Canada's mixed forest. This forest fringes the Great Lakes and spreads eastward along the St. Lawrence River valley to the Atlantic Ocean. Here we see evergreens as well as broad-leafed trees that shed their leaves in winter. The important trees are pine, spruce, hemlock, maple, birch, and aspen.* They are used for wood pulp and for timber. We see many acres of farmland from which the trees have been cleared. In the winter, many farmers cut logs on their farms or work in logging camps.

A newsprint rolling machine. Canada produces more newsprint paper than any other country.

The forest-products industry. More Canadian workers earn their living in the forest-products industry than in any other industry. Many of these people work in pulp and paper mills where newsprint is made. Canada produces more newsprint than any other country in the world. Most of it is exported to the United States. Perhaps the newspaper your family reads is printed on paper made in Canadian mills.

Much of the lumber cut in the sawmills is sold outside Canada. The money from these exports helps Canadians buy the products they need from other countries. Not only are trees used for wood pulp and lumber, but also for making alcohol, plywood, rayon, fertilizer, and many other products.

In Canadian research centers, scientists are learning new and better ways of using their country's forests. They study the treatment of tree diseases in order to keep the forests healthy. These men are also discovering new uses for wood, so that no part of a tree will be wasted.

---DO YOU KNOW---

1. On the map on page 64, locate Canada's three main forest regions.
2. Find pictures that show how logs are taken from the forests to sawmills.
3. What different kinds of trees are mentioned in this chapter?
4. List some products of Canadian forests other than wood pulp and lumber.

A research center. Canadian scientists are experimenting with new ways of controlling tree diseases.

Drying codfish. The cleaned, salted fish are spread out on wooden platforms called "flakes."

CHAPTER SEVEN

FISHING AND FURS

Fishing on the Atlantic Coast of Canada. Let us walk down the street of a fishing village in Newfoundland.* Near the docks we see several fishermen mending their nets. In the harbor is a fleet of schooners* that have just returned from a three-week trip to the Grand Banks.* (See map on page 11.) The ocean is shallow at the Grand Banks. These shallow waters provide good feeding grounds

69

Fishing off the Grand Banks.* Fishermen raise a bag-shaped net full of fish into their trawler.*

Packing sardines. Many canneries in eastern Canada prepare fish for shipment to other countries

for millions of fish. We watch the fishermen unload kegs of salted codfish from the schooners. They spread the cleaned, salted fish on long wooden platforms, called "flakes," to dry. (See picture on page 69.)

Anchored in the harbor are several wide, sturdy-looking boats called trawlers. These boats are usually powered by steam or diesel* engines. Fishermen are unloading barrels of haddock, hake,* pollack,* and halibut from the trawlers. The fish were caught in large, bag-shaped nets that were lowered over the sides of the fishing vessels. Then the nets were dragged slowly along the bottom of the sea.

The smaller motorboats that we see are used for fishing within a few miles of the shore. "Inshore fishermen" use nets and hand lines to catch herring, mackerel, cod, and haddock. Near the docks a lobster fisherman is emptying his traps. Many shellfish are caught in the shallow waters along the coast.

Setting a salmon net. Fishermen along Canada's Pacific Coast catch millions of salmon each year.

Men have been catching fish in Canada for many years. More than 450 years ago, John Cabot, an explorer who sailed from England, discovered the rich fishing grounds on the Grand Banks. Fishermen in Europe heard of his discovery, and began to come to the Grand Banks on fishing voyages. Later, men built villages along the coast. Today, fishing is one of the most important industries along the Atlantic Coast between Newfoundland and the southern tip of Nova Scotia.* (See map on page 11.) Nearly 80,000 Canadians earn their living from the sea.

Fishing along the Pacific Coast. Let us leave Newfoundland and travel west to the Pacific Coast. We board a boat at the mouth

Inside a fish cannery. Nearly eighty thousand Canadians earn their living from the sea.

Fishing on Lake Erie. The Great Lakes are among the world's largest fresh-water fisheries.

of the Fraser River in British Columbia.* Hundreds of fishermen have anchored their small boats near us. The summer sun shines on nets full of silvery salmon, which the men are hauling into their boats.

The life habits of salmon make them easy to catch. They are born in quiet inland streams and lakes. Later, they swim downstream to the ocean where they live for about four years. Then great schools of salmon fight their way back up the rivers to lay their eggs. It is easy to catch these fish on their journey up the river.

The Canadian government has wisely set aside certain weeks of the year when no salmon fishing is permitted. During these closed

Ice fishing. To catch fish in winter, Canadian fishermen lower nets through holes in the ice.

seasons the fish swim safely upstream and lay their eggs. There are also many fish hatcheries in Canada. Here the eggs are hatched and the tiny fish are fed until they are large enough to be set free. For these reasons, Canada's west coast fisheries continue to yield millions of pounds of salmon every year.

Much of the salmon caught along the west coast is canned. On a visit to a fish cannery, we watch machines clean the salmon and cut them into pieces. The pieces of fish are then packed in cans

74

and cooked in pressure cookers. Canada sends fresh, canned, and frozen fish to markets all over the world.

Fishing on Canada's rivers and lakes. Now we are fishing from a small boat on the clear, cold waters of Lake Winnipeg. (See map on page 11.) Near us we see several other fishermen in rowboats and motorboats. They are reeling in whitefish, pickerel, pike, and tullibee.* There are also many large commercial fishing boats on the lake. If we were here in winter, we would see men lowering nets through holes in the ice to catch fish. Canada's inland lakes and rivers are the largest fresh-water fisheries in the world.

Fur trappers and fur farms. During the long winter, Indian and white trappers set their traps for mink, muskrat, fox, beaver,

Deep-freezing trays of packaged fish. Canada sends frozen fish all over the world.

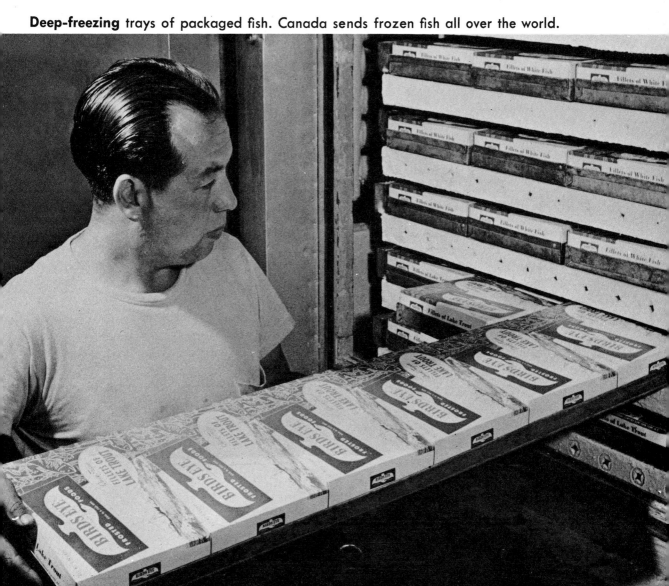

squirrel, and ermine. Next they clean and stretch these valuable pelts. In summer, when the ice on Canada's streams and rivers has melted, the trappers bring boatloads of furs to the nearest trading posts. These furs and those from almost 2,500 Canadian fur farms are then sent to markets in many parts of the world.

---DO YOU KNOW---

1. Select pictures in this chapter that describe different ways of fishing.
2. About how many Canadians earn their living from the sea?
3. Why are there certain weeks in Canada when no salmon fishing is permitted?
4. What valuable furs are sent from Canada to markets in many parts of the world?

Inspecting silver fox furs. Valuable pelts from Canada's fur farms are shipped to many lands.

A reservoir.* Water from Canada's lakes and rivers is used to produce hydroelectric* power.

CHAPTER EIGHT
NATURAL RESOURCES AND INDUSTRY

Canada has many natural resources. Thousands of lakes and swiftly flowing rivers produce hydroelectric* power for industry. Dense, green forests and rich mineral deposits provide raw materials for mills and factories. Canada's water power, forests, and minerals have helped to make her one of the leading industrial nations of the world.

Water power. One of Canada's most important natural resources is water power. In the nation's hydroelectric plants, rushing water turns large turbines* to produce electric power. This electric power runs the machinery in three fourths of the factories in

77

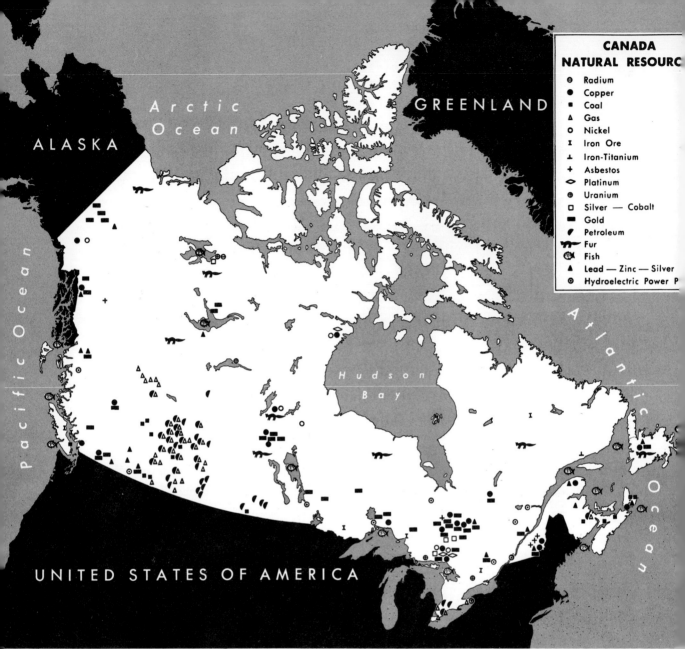

The legend on the map reads:

CANADA
NATURAL RESOURC[ES]

- ⊖ Radium
- ● Copper
- ■ Coal
- ▲ Gas
- ○ Nickel
- ⊥ Iron Ore
- ⊥ Iron-Titanium
- + Asbestos
- ⬦ Platinum
- ⊕ Uranium
- ▢ Silver — Cobalt
- ▬ Gold
- ◗ Petroleum
- Fur
- Fish
- ▲ Lead — Zinc — Silver
- ⊙ Hydroelectric Power P[lants]

Canada's natural resources have helped to make her a leading industrial nation.

Canada. Several of the world's largest hydroelectric plants have been built in the province of Quebec.* (See map above.) The Beauharnois* plant near Montreal is the largest of these.

Petroleum* and natural gas.* Two other important sources of power in Canada are petroleum and natural gas. Just over ten years ago, large deposits of petroleum were discovered in the Western Plains. Since then, more and more oil has been found.

Today, it is Canada's most valuable mineral. Natural gas was discovered during the search for petroleum. Gas is now used in homes and in industry. Giant pipelines carry gas and oil to many parts of Canada and to the United States.

Coal. Although there are large coal fields in Canada, only a few of the nation's factories use Canadian coal. Much of Canada's coal is of poor quality. Also, most of it is located very far from her mills and factories. Because many of Canada's industries are near coal fields in the United States, it is often cheaper for Canada to import coal from her neighbor than to mine it herself.

Iron ore. Canada has many rich iron mines. (See map on page 78.) One of the most interesting mines is at Knob Lake, on the Quebec-Labrador border. Until 1942 this was a quiet wilderness. Although geologists* had known for more than sixty years that there was

Drilling for oil, Canada's most valuable mineral. There are many oil wells on the Western Plains.

iron ore in this region, no one had been interested in mining it. Then, in 1942, a mining company claimed the land. Before the mine could be opened, airplanes had to bring men and supplies to this remote location. Then it was necessary to build a railroad through this desolate area. Three hundred and sixty miles of railroad tracks were laid north from the St. Lawrence River to the Quebec-Labrador border. Loading docks were built along the coast at the southern end of the railroad. Here, ore from the mines could be loaded onto ships. The town of Knob Lake grew up at the northern end of the railroad. A power plant was built on a river nearby, to provide electric power for the town and the mine. Today, much of the iron ore mined at Knob Lake is exported to the United States.

The Steep Rock * **iron mine.** A lake was drained to reach ore deposits in this mine.

Packing asbestos* into bags. Canada produces most of the world's supply of this rock fiber.

The mines at Steep Rock, Ontario, also produce large quantities of iron ore. Steep Rock Lake was drained to reach the valuable iron ore deposits which lay beneath the water. If we were to fly over these mines, we would see below us a rust-colored canyon in the middle of the wilderness.

Copper. Another of Canada's leading minerals is copper. Much of the copper dug from Canadian mines is exported to other countries. Let us travel to the large copper mines at Sudbury, Ontario, where nearly half of Canada's copper is mined. Not far from the mines we see the high chimneys of the smelters* in which the copper ore is refined. Fumes from the smelters have withered all the trees and grass nearby. Towering mounds of waste material rise on all sides.

Nickel. On our visit to Sudbury we see much nickel being processed, since ores that contain copper usually contain nickel as well. Canada is the world's leading producer of this metal. Much of Canada's nickel is melted with iron to make high-quality steel.

Gold. Now we travel more than a hundred miles north of Sudbury to one of the largest gold mines in the world. This is the giant Hollinger Mine. From this and other gold mines in Canada comes about one sixth of the world's supply of gold.

Canadian industries. Canada is one of the leading industrial nations in the world.

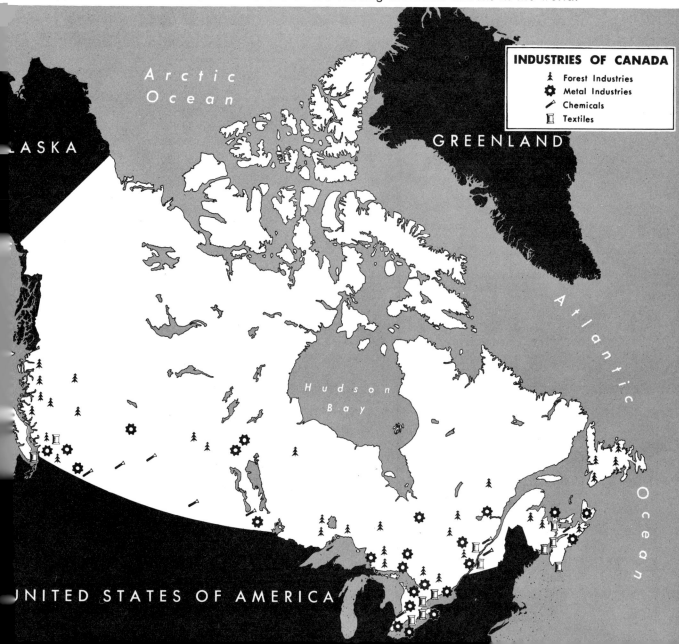

INDUSTRIES OF CANADA

🌲 Forest Industries
⚙ Metal Industries
⚒ Chemicals
🧵 Textiles

Arctic Ocean

ALASKA

GREENLAND

Hudson Bay

Atlantic Ocean

UNITED STATES OF AMERICA

Platinum. Another precious metal mined in Canada is platinum. Because this metal is not harmed by most acids and can withstand high temperatures, it is used by dentists, jewelers, surgeons, and chemists. Canada is one of the world's leading producers of platinum.

Asbestos. Canada is a leading producer of one of the world's most amazing minerals, asbestos. Because this greenish rock fiber will not burn, it is used to make fireproof wallboard, shingles, and other building materials. Canada's asbestos is usually dug from large open pits.

An automobile factory. Many United States car manufacturers have factories in Canada.

Pouring molten aluminum into molds. Canada is the world's second largest producer of aluminum.

Uranium. Large deposits of uranium have recently been discovered in Canada. Uranium has become a very valuable mineral, for it is used in harnessing atomic energy.

The metal industry. Canadians have built many mills and factories to process the minerals taken from their country's rich mines. Today, the manufacture of iron and steel is an important branch of Canada's metal industry. Many iron and steel mills are located around the port city of Hamilton, on the western shore of Lake Ontario. (See map on page 11.) Ships loaded with iron ore and coal for these mills sail through the Great Lakes to this port. Other ships carry bars of pig iron and sheets of steel from Hamilton to other Canadian cities. There, these materials are manufactured into pipes, rails, ships, and other goods.

In a Canadian chemical plant. Crude oil is used in making plastics, paint, and other products.

The manufacture of automobiles is another important part of Canada's metal industry. Many United States car manufacturers have factories in Canada. The city of Windsor, on the western tip of Lake Erie, is called the "Detroit of Canada" because so many automobile factories are located there.

Another important part of Canada's metal industry is the smelting and refining of metals that do not contain iron. These metals are called nonferrous metals. Canada is second only to the United States in the production of aluminum, one of the most important nonferrous metals. This is surprising, because Canada does not have any of the reddish, claylike ore in which aluminum is found. This ore is brought to Canada by ship from British Guiana* and Jamaica.*

Large amounts of electricity are needed in refining aluminum. Canada's giant hydroelectric plants can produce this power cheaply. The large Shipshaw power station at Arvida* supplies electricity for a giant aluminum smelter in Quebec. This is one of the two largest and most modern aluminum smelters in the world. The other is at Kitimat, British Columbia. (See map on page 11.)

The chemical industry. We usually think of petroleum as being used to make gasoline. However, scientists have learned to make many other valuable products from this mineral. In Canadian chemical plants, workers make medicines, sulphur, paints, plastics, and other products from crude petroleum. Most of these chemical plants are located near large oil refineries.

A clothing factory. The manufacture of clothing is the main branch of Canada's textile industry.

The textile industry. The manufacture of clothing is the most important branch of Canada's textile industry. A large number of textile and clothing factories are found in towns in southern Quebec and Ontario, where many workers are available. Rivers near these towns provide cheap electricity to run the machines.

The food industry. Many Canadians work in food-processing plants throughout Canada. Here they prepare foods for use in Canada and for export to other countries. Flour is the main processed food which Canada exports.

====DO YOU KNOW====

1. With the aid of pictures in this chapter, list several natural resources of Canada.
2. On the map on page 78, locate the important minerals found in Canada.

3. Using the map on page 83, list Canada's leading industries.
4. Name some valuable petroleum products made in Canadian chemical plants.

Preparing meat for market. Many Canadians work in food-processing plants throughout the country

Loading flour at Montreal.* Ocean-going ships travel up the St. Lawrence River to this port.

CHAPTER NINE

TRANSPORTATION AND COMMUNICATION

Canada's waterways. Since earliest times the people of Canada have made good use of their country's many waterways. Indians once paddled canoes over the rivers and along the shores of the Great Lakes. Later, fur traders and early settlers used the same waterways. Their most important water route was the St. Lawrence

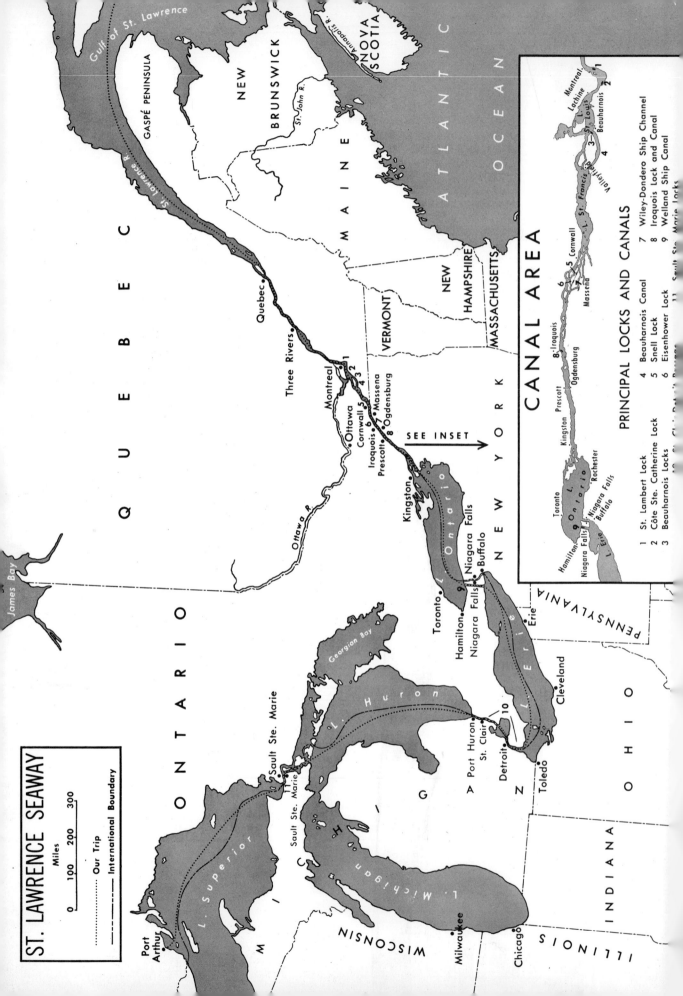

ST. LAWRENCE SEAWAY

Miles

0   100   200   300

.... Our Trip
— — — International Boundary

CANAL AREA

PRINCIPAL LOCKS AND CANALS

1   St. Lambert Lock
2   Côte Ste. Catherine Lock
3   Beauharnois Locks

4   Beauharnois Canal
5   Snell Lock
6   Eisenhower Lock

7   Wiley-Dondero Ship Channel
8   Iroquois Lock and Canal
9   Welland Ship Canal

SEE INSET ➡

Gulf of St. Lawrence

GASPÉ PENINSULA

NEW BRUNSWICK

NOVA SCOTIA

Annapolis R.

St. John R.

MAINE

ATLANTIC OCEAN

QUEBEC

Quebec

Three Rivers

Montreal
Ottawa
Cornwall
Massena
Iroquois
Prescott
Ogdensburg
Kingston

Ottawa R.

VERMONT

NEW HAMPSHIRE

MASSACHUSETTS

NEW YORK

L. Ontario

Toronto
Hamilton
Niagara Falls
Buffalo
Erie

James Bay

ONTARIO

Georgian Bay

Sault Ste. Marie
Sault Ste. Marie

L. Superior

Port Arthur

L. Huron

L. Michigan

L. Erie

Cleveland

Port Huron
St. Clair
Detroit
Toledo

PENNSYLVANIA

OHIO

INDIANA

ILLINOIS

WISCONSIN

MICHIGAN

Milwaukee
Chicago

Montreal
Lachine
St. Louis
Beauharnois
Valleyfield
L. St. Francis
Cornwall
Massena
Iroquois
Ogdensburg
Prescott
Kingston
Toronto
L. Ontario
Rochester
Niagara Falls
Hamilton
Niagara Falls
Buffalo
L. Erie

The St. Lawrence Seaway is the greatest inland waterway in the world. It extends for miles along the St. Lawrence River and through the Great Lakes.

River. Today, this great river is a part of the St. Lawrence Seaway, the greatest inland water-highway in the world. (See map on page 90.)

Imagine that you are aboard a large ship that has just sailed from the Atlantic Ocean into the Gulf of St. Lawrence. You are going to travel more than 2,200 miles along the St. Lawrence River and through the Great Lakes to the western end of Lake Superior. On the way you will pass through many canals and great locks* that will raise the ship in giant steps to 602 feet above the level of the Atlantic Ocean. They will allow your ship to sail safely around swift rapids and rushing waterfalls.

After traveling for about one thousand miles, you stop for a short time at the port of Montreal.* The rapids between Montreal and the Great Lakes once prevented ships from going farther up

Niagara Falls. The Welland Ship Canal bypasses these falls and links Lake Erie to Lake Ontario.

the river. Now locks and canals along the way make it possible for you to continue your trip. Soon your ship enters the blue waters of Lake Ontario, and you sail on toward Lake Erie.

The Niagara River forms a natural water link between Lake Ontario and Lake Erie. (See map on page 11.) Your ship cannot use this river, however, because of the giant Niagara Falls. Here waters of the Niagara River crash down more than 150 feet on their way to Lake Ontario. You bypass these falls by sailing through a canal that connects Lake Ontario and Lake Erie. This is the twenty-seven-mile-long Welland Canal, which raises your ship 326 feet to the level of Lake Erie.

Now you cross Lake Erie and travel through the St. Clair–Detroit Passage into Lake Huron. You sail northwest across this lake to the canals and locks at Sault Ste. Marie.* These locks

Loading grain onto ships. Many Canadian ships on the Great Lakes carry iron ore and wheat.

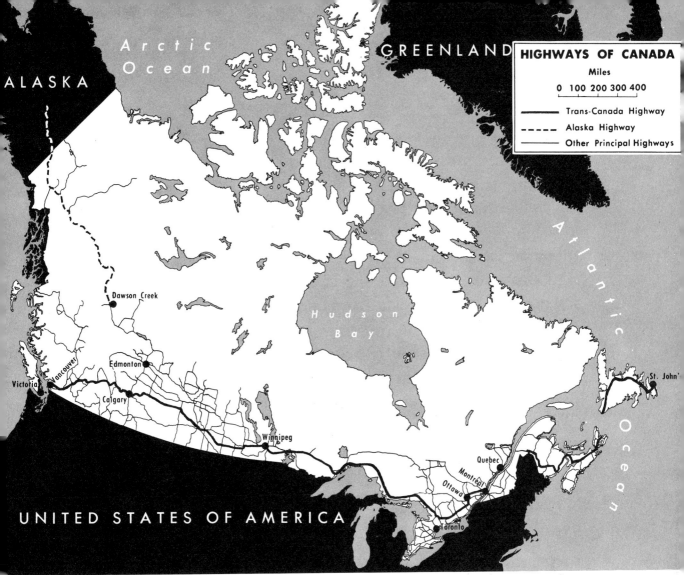

A network of highways covers southern Canada. The Trans-Canada Highway crosses the country.

raise the ship to the waters of Lake Superior. As you sail across Lake Superior you see many other large ships. Some of them carry wheat. Many are loaded with iron ore. Finally your ship docks at Port Arthur, on the northwestern shore of Lake Superior.

Highways. You continue west from Port Arthur on the Trans-Canada Highway. (See map above.) This great highway begins at St. John's, on the eastern coast of Newfoundland.* It ends at Victoria,* on Canada's west coast. The Trans-Canada Highway is nearly 4,500 miles long. Construction workers built many new roads, and joined them with old ones to form this highway. They moved millions of tons of rock, filled in marshland, and built hundreds of bridges along the way. The Trans-Canada Highway is the most important of Canada's many good roads.

Now you reach the city of Calgary* in the province of Alberta.* Here you turn off the Trans-Canada Highway and take a road that leads northwest to Dawson Creek, in the province of British Columbia.*

At Dawson Creek, you begin to travel over the Alaska Highway. This road was built by the United States during World War II. It has since been lengthened and improved. Travelers may now

The Queen Elizabeth Highway is one of the many good roads that crisscross southern Canada.

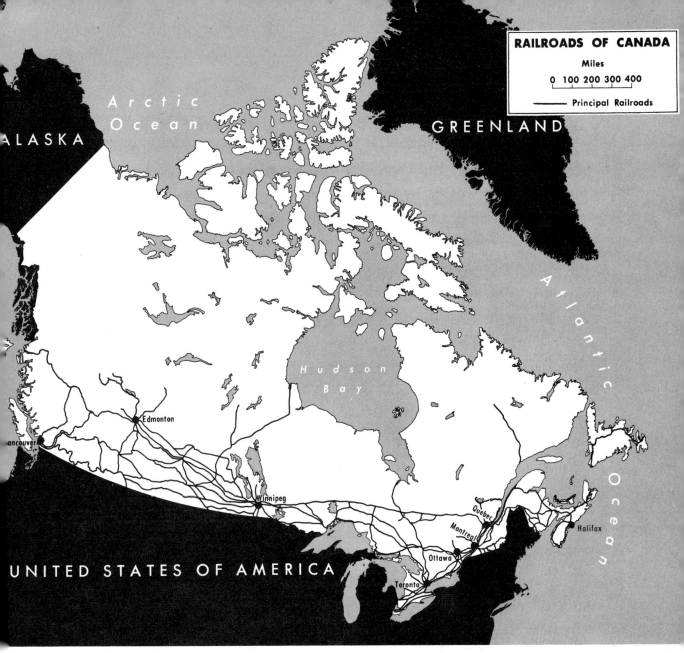

Canada's railroads are in the southern part of the country. They link the east and west coasts.

follow the Alaska Highway for more than fourteen hundred miles, into the heart of Alaska. (See map on page 93.)

Railways. November 7, 1885, was an exciting day in Canada. Workmen, businessmen, and officials from many parts of the country gathered in Eagle Pass in British Columbia. They came to watch Lord Strathcona* drive the last spike in the track of Canada's first transcontinental railroad.

A streamliner in the Rockies. Only the United States and Russia have more miles of railroad than Canada.

For several years before this day, thousands of men worked hard to build this railroad. They laid steel tracks across Canada's plains and up steep grades of the Rocky Mountains. They built bridges across rivers and deep canyons.

Some of the first people to use this railroad were settlers going to build new homes on Canada's vast prairies. Within a few years freight trains roared back to the east coast carrying wheat from the new farms. Workmen in the east loaded the trains with manufactured goods for the prairie farmers. As the prairie settlements grew, more railroads were built. These connected the settlements with towns on Canada's east and west coasts.

Airplanes and dog sleds carry mail, medical aid, and supplies to people in northern Canada.

Today, Canada's railroads are operated mainly by the Canadian National and the Canadian Pacific railroad companies. Canada uses more railway transportation per person than any other country in the world. Only the United States and Russia have more miles of railroad tracks.

Canadian airlines. Airplanes are used in many ways in Canada. Forest rangers, fish conservationists, and Royal Canadian Mounted Police officers inspect their territories from the air. During the summer, geologists in northern Canada often use helicopters to

Air routes connect many Canadian cities. They also link Canada to other countries of the world.

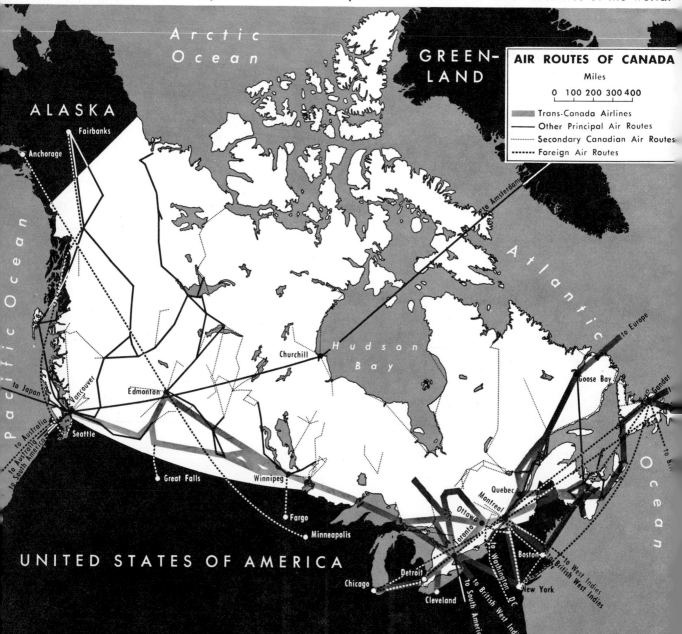

AIR ROUTES OF CANADA

Miles

0 100 200 300 400

Trans-Canada Airlines
Other Principal Air Routes
Secondary Canadian Air Routes
Foreign Air Routes

Boarding an airliner. Several Canadian airlines fly over the North Atlantic to Europe.

map the areas in which they may find different types of rock. Many people in the far north use airplanes to fly in medical aid, supplies, and mail.

From the Malton Airport just outside Toronto,* you can fly to many Canadian cities and to foreign countries. Several Canadian airlines now fly regularly over the North Atlantic to Europe. From central and western Canada, planes fly to Europe on a route which crosses the Arctic Circle.*

Communications. Airplanes, trains, ships, and dog sleds help carry mail to every corner of Canada. The two main railroad companies and the government operate telegraph systems that reach all parts of the country. Good newspapers, magazines, and radio programs bring Canadians news and entertainment. The Canadian Broadcasting Corporation sends shortwave broadcasts in sixteen languages to Europe and to other parts of the world. Canadians also enjoy television programs produced in both the French and English languages.

---DO YOU KNOW---

1. Find pictures in this chapter that show ways in which people travel in Canada.
2. Using maps and pictures in this chapter, describe Canada's transportation system.
3. What famous waterfalls are located between Lake Ontario and Lake Erie?
4. In what different ways are airplanes used in Canada?

A television control room. Canadians enjoy news and entertainment over radio and television.

Quebec* was founded by French traders in 1608. Part of the city is built on a high cliff.

CHAPTER TEN
CITIES OF CANADA

You could travel for hundreds of miles in Canada and never see a large city. This vast country has only twelve cities of more than 150,000 people. All of these are in southern Canada, where there are important industries and rich farmlands. Let us travel through the southern part of the country and visit some Canadian cities.

Quebec.* We begin our trip in old Quebec. This city is located along the St. Lawrence River about eight hundred miles from the Atlantic Ocean. (See map on page 11.) Quebec was founded as a French trading post in 1608. It was the second permanent settlement in Canada. Now about 310,000 people live here. Part of Quebec

The Citadel. This stone fortress was built to guard the city of Quebec against enemy attack.

is built on a cliff that rises more than three hundred feet above the river. This is called "Upper Town." The other part of the city is known as "Lower Town." It spreads along a narrow strip of land between the cliff and the river.

Most of the older homes, churches, shops, and public buildings of Quebec are in Upper Town. At the very top of the cliff we see the Citadel, a great stone fortress that was built to guard the city from enemy attack. Another interesting building is the Château Frontenac.* This is a large hotel built in the style of a French castle. From the hotel we can see much of Lower Town and the harbor. Steep stairways and narrow, winding streets lead from Upper Town to the lower part of the city. Here buildings and houses are crowded close together.

102

Many of the people of Quebec earn their living by working in paper mills and clothing factories. Others are employed in tobacco factories, tanneries, and brickyards.

Montreal.* Now we board a ship and sail about 160 miles up the St. Lawrence to Montreal, Canada's largest city. (See map on page 11.) Montreal was founded more than three hundred years ago as a small French settlement. Today, over a million and a half people live in this great city. We notice that the greater part of Montreal is on an island, which is joined to the mainland by several bridges. A large forest-covered hill rises in the center of the city. This is Mount Royal. If we climb to the top of Mount Royal and look toward the river, we can see Montreal's industrial

Montreal* is Canada's largest city and leading seaport. It is on the St. Lawrence River.

and business centers. Below us, on the lower slope of the hill, the trees are so thick they hide the many houses built there.

Montreal is the most important manufacturing city in Canada. Electrical goods, railroad equipment, and clothing are produced in its factories. There are many sugar refineries in the city. Near the docks along the river, we see large grain elevators and flour mills. Although Montreal is located about a thousand miles from the Atlantic Ocean, it is the largest and most important seaport in Canada.

Ottawa.* About one hundred miles west of Montreal is Ottawa, the capital city of Canada. (See map on page 11.) We reach this

Ottawa* is the capital of Canada. Part of the city is on a hill overlooking the Ottawa River.

he **Rideau Canal*** flows through the heart of Ottawa. Many fine homes are built along this canal.

beautiful city after a two-hour train ride from Montreal. On a hill overlooking the Ottawa River are three large stone buildings. These are the Parliament buildings, where the laws of Canada are made. Rising high above these buildings is the famous Peace Tower.*

As we ride through the streets of the city, we see lovely parks and gardens. Many fine homes are located along the Rideau Canal,* which flows through the heart of Ottawa. (See picture above.) In the northeastern part of the city, near the Ottawa River, is Rockcliffe Park. It covers about one hundred acres. Near this park, we pass the residences of the Canadian Prime Minister* and the Governor General, and the homes of several foreign ambassadors.

Toronto* is on the northwestern shore of Lake Ontario. It is Canada's second largest city.

Ottawa began as a lumbering town about 150 years ago. Today about 350,000 people live here. Many people in Ottawa work for the government.

Toronto.* A short bus ride from Ottawa brings us to the small port city of Kingston, on Lake Ontario. Here we board a Great Lakes steamer bound for Toronto, the second largest city in Canada. Nearly 1,400,000 people live in this city. Toronto is located on the northwestern shore of Lake Ontario. (See map on page 11.) As we sail into the harbor, we see coal docks, warehouses, and railroad yards along the shore. North of the harbor are the commercial and industrial sections of the city. Toronto

106

is the second most important manufacturing city in Canada. It is the printing and publishing center for the entire country. From Toronto's factories come electrical goods, metal products, and food products.

As we travel around Toronto, we notice that all the houses are made of brick, stone, or stucco.* City fire laws state that people may not build wooden houses.

Winnipeg.* Now we board a fast train and travel west to the city of Winnipeg. (See map on page 11.) More than 400,000 people live in this plains city. It is the fourth largest city in Canada. Winnipeg is the main trading center for eastern and western Canada.

Winnipeg* is the largest city on the Western Plains. It is an important meat-packing center.

All transcontinental rail traffic passes through the city. We see trains from eastern Canada loaded with manufactured goods and with imported products such as automobiles and coffee. Other trains are carrying cattle and grain from western Canada.

Not far from the railroad station are many large buildings. One of these is the Winnipeg Grain Exchange. Here men come to buy and sell wheat and other grains. Just east of the city, we pass western Canada's largest meat-packing plants. Meat packing is Winnipeg's leading industry. Many people also work in flour mills, dairies, and railroad repair shops.

Vancouver.* Finally, we visit Vancouver, a city on the Pacific Coast. (See map on page 11.) Although Vancouver is less than a hundred years old, it is already the third largest city in Canada.

Transcontinental trains must pass through Winnipeg on their way across the country.

Vancouver,* Canada's third largest city, is the country's leading port on the Pacific Coast.

Its excellent harbor has helped to make Vancouver the most important Canadian port on the Pacific Coast. As we walk along the water front, we see large freighters being loaded with wheat, wood pulp, lumber, apples, and canned fish. A large suspension bridge stretches across the entrance to the harbor. It is more than fifteen hundred feet long. The business and industrial sections of Vancouver are located near the harbor. Many people here work in foundries,* sawmills, sugar refineries, oil refineries, and canning plants.

─────────────DO YOU KNOW─────────────

1. Using pictures and the text, describe the old city of Quebec.
2. List industries which help to make Montreal a leading manufacturing city.
3. Name the capital city of Canada. What famous places are located in this city?
4. What is Canada's most important port city on the Pacific coast?

An Eskimo carving made of soapstone.* The Indians and Eskimos were Canada's first artists.

CHAPTER ELEVEN
ARTS AND CRAFTS

Eskimo and Indian art. Canada's first artists were the Eskimos and Indians. Long ago, Eskimos carved beautiful objects from ivory and stone. Often they carved figures of people. They also made many carvings of animals. Some of the small animal figures were made to represent the good spirits* of their religion. Others were made for Eskimo children to use as toys.

Eskimo artists still carve many interesting figures of people and animals. Today, they make most of them from a very soft kind of stone called soapstone.* Eskimo carvings are very simple and lovely in design. Sometimes they do not look exactly like the people or animals they represent. They may give the outline of the figure without including small details. (See picture on page 110.)

The Canadian government is encouraging the Eskimos to make more carvings. It is helping the Eskimos sell these works of art to people in Canada and in other countries of the world.

For many centuries the Indians on Canada's Pacific Coast were excellent artists. They carved beautiful and useful objects from the wood of giant cedar trees. They made totem* poles, canoes, boxes, pipes, and many other articles. Most of these objects were

Painting a totem* pole. Pacific Coast Indians carved many objects from the wood of cedar trees.

carved in the shapes of animals, birds, and sometimes men. Often they were painted in bright colors.

As the Indians learned to live like their white neighbors, fewer of them took time for these handicrafts. Today, only a few Pacific Coast Indians carve as beautifully as their ancestors did. However, we can see the works of earlier Indian artists in many Canadian museums.

Weaving and other handicrafts are taught in special craft schools in some parts of Canada.

French-Canadian wood carver. Early French settlers carved statues of saints for their churches.

Homecrafts of the Canadians. The early Europeans who came to Canada had little time for art. Their only idle hours came during the long Canadian winters. These settlers spent many winter evenings around the family fireplace, making beautiful articles to use in their homes. The women wove soft, brightly colored cloth, which they made into blankets and clothing. Leftover bits of cloth were used to make gay hooked rugs. Sometimes the men carved wooden statues of saints for their churches.

Today, some families in Quebec* and the Maritime Region still make beautiful articles in their homes. In Quebec, there are special

"Blackfoot Chief and Subordinates" is one of Paul Kane's* many paintings of Canadian Indians

craft schools where people learn to work with clay, metal, and leather. Here too, they learn to spin and weave. These home-crafts are displayed in large exhibits, where they are sold to Canadians and to tourists.

Canadian painters. Very few pictures were painted in Canada before the nineteenth century. To see the works of Canadian painters since that time, let us join the people who are visiting the National Gallery in the city of Ottawa.*

The first room we enter is filled with colorful paintings which show the life and adventures of Canada's early Indians. We pause

114

before a picture of tall, stern-faced warriors, clothed in their bright tribal dress. The artist has painted this picture so realistically that it looks almost like a color photograph. In the painting, we see each detail of the Indians' clothing, their tepees, the cloudy sky, and the lonely western plain upon which they lived. The metal plate beneath the picture tells us that "Blackfoot Chief and Subordinates" was painted by Paul Kane* about 1848. Kane traveled west to the plains, visiting several tribes of Indians along the way. He painted the rugged countryside and the Indians just as he had seen them.

Another artist who painted the Canadian countryside just as he saw it was Cornelius Krieghoff,* from Holland. Krieghoff painted scenes of village and country life in nineteenth-century Quebec.

As time went on, many Canadian artists began painting the Canadian landscape in simple, bold outlines and bright colors. These pictures did not look at all like photographs. James Morrice* was one of Canada's first artists to paint in this way. Morrice spent much of his life in other countries. However, some later Canadian artists were strongly influenced by his style of painting.

In the Art Gallery of Toronto,* we see the works of some of Canada's twentieth-century artists. In one room hangs the painting "St. Hilarion, Quebec," by A. Y. Jackson.* This is a winter scene in which small village houses are painted against a lonely background of white snow. Looking closely, we see that the artist used bold brush strokes in painting the picture. Jackson was one of a group of seven Canadian artists who were interested in painting the Canadian landscape in a colorful, free manner. Some of these artists traveled far into the Canadian Shield. They painted the wild forests, lakes, and rugged hills of this part of Canada. The first exhibition of paintings by the "Group of Seven"* in

1920 was not successful. Canadians at that time did not appreciate the work of the seven artists. Today, however, most Canadians enjoy these colorful, exciting pictures.

Music in Canada. Canadians enjoy many kinds of music. Ten symphony orchestras present concerts which are well attended and well supported financially by the people. Many young students attend these concerts, for they have learned to appreciate music in their schools. There are also several fine choirs in Toronto, Montreal,* and other Canadian cities. At the Winnipeg Music Festival,* we hear soloists, orchestras, and choirs perform after many hours of preparation. Scholarships and prizes are awarded to talented young musicians at this and other musical festivals.

"St. Hilarion, Quebec," by A. Y. Jackson* is a bold, free painting of the Canadian countryside.

A symphony orchestra. People in most large Canadian cities can attend symphony concerts.

Plays and ballet. Now we enter the beautiful new theater in Stratford,* Ontario. As we take our seats, the lights in the auditorium begin to dim. The hum of voices from the audience is hushed as the curtain slowly rises. On the dimly lit stage, we see the gray stone walls of an ancient castle. The sentries guarding the walls speak in frightened voices of a strange ghost they have seen. We are watching the opening scene of *Hamlet,* a famous play by William Shakespeare. Plays by Shakespeare are presented at the Stratford Shakespearean Festival each year. This world-famous drama* festival attracts many people.

In addition to the theater at Stratford, there are excellent theater groups in many other Canadian cities. Good plays are also broadcast over television and radio. Many people also attend the performances of Canada's fine new ballet companies.

117

Literature in Canada. In Canada's libraries, we find that many of the books are written in French, although most are written in English. French-Canadian and British-Canadian novelists and poets have written colorful accounts of Canada's history. They have vividly described the natural beauties of their vast homeland and have written humorous and thrilling tales of the wild Canadian frontier. You would probably enjoy reading Robert Service's* famous ballad, "The Shooting of Dan McGrew," and the novel, *Anne of Green Gables,* by Lucy M. Montgomery.*

---DO YOU KNOW---

1. Find pictures to help describe the art work of Indians and Eskimos in Canada.
2. What kind of paintings were made by the "Group of Seven"?
3. Describe the painting "St. Hilarion, Quebec" shown on page 116.
4. Describe the many kinds of music which the people of Canada enjoy.

The plays of William Shakespeare are produced every summer in Stratford,* Ontario.

People swim and sun-bathe in Canada's many lakes during the long, warm days of summer.

CHAPTER TWELVE
SPORTS AND RECREATION

In Canada, each new season brings with it the excitement and fun of different sports and recreation. Canadians play and watch many kinds of games. They are an active, outdoor people and enjoy their rugged, beautiful country no matter what the time of year.

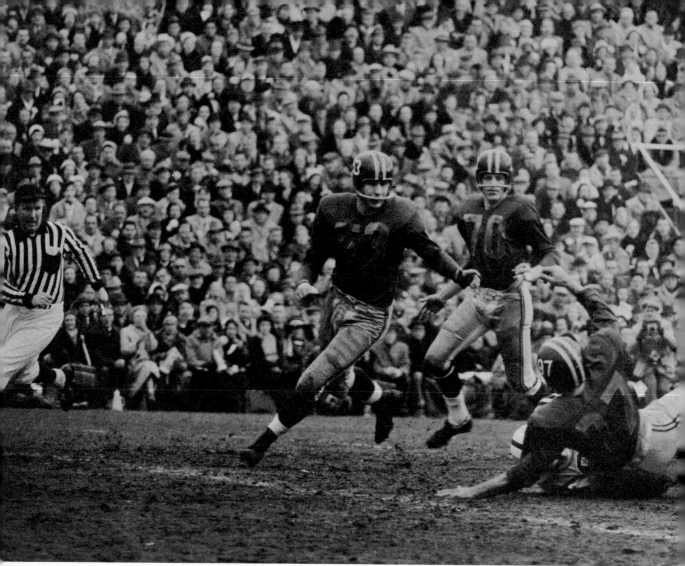

A football game. Canadian football fields are larger than those in the United States.

Football. On crisp, fall week ends, students in Canadian high schools and colleges watch their school teams play football. Thousands of other people crowd into stadiums in the large cities to watch games played by professional football players.

Canadians play football in nearly the same way as people in the United States play the game. In Canada, however, the football field is longer and wider. Also, there is one more player on each team.

Ice hockey. Wherever you go in the fall and winter you may see people playing or watching ice hockey. Ice hockey is Canada's national sport. Nearly eighty thousand Canadian men and boys play on organized hockey teams. There are professional teams in some of the large cities.

Ice hockey is a fast, difficult game. Only expert skaters can play the game well. It is not by chance that some of the finest hockey players in the world are Canadians. Children learn to ice skate very early in this land of long, cold winters. Most people skate on outdoor rinks in cities, towns, and villages. There are skating clubs for both children and adults. These clubs sponsor skating contests.

Ice hockey is a fast, difficult game. Some of the world's best hockey players are Canadians.

Curling. Curling is an interesting sport also played on ice rinks in Canada. (See picture below.) In this game, each team has four players. They take turns sliding large, smooth stones towards a mark at each end of the rink. These marks are located in the center of three circles which look like the rings on a target. To score, stones must be within one of the circles. A point is scored for each stone that slides nearer to the mark than any stone belonging to the other team.

Curling. In this game, players slide stones over the ice towards a mark at the end of the rink.

Many Canadians enjoy skiing. Children learn to ski in classes sponsored by schools or ski clubs.

Skiing. Another winter sport which many Canadians enjoy is skiing. Some of the country's best ski runs are in Quebec,* Ontario,* and the western mountains. (See map on page 11.) On winter week ends in these parts of Canada, trains and highways are crowded with skiers bound for nearby ski slopes or mountain resorts. Children learn to ski in classes sponsored by schools and ski clubs. Skiers compete in racing, cross-country trail skiing, and ski jumping. There are many long ski trails through the woods in eastern Canada. Skiers often take day-long trips on these.

Snowshoeing. Perhaps the most unusual winter sport in Canada is snowshoeing. Long ago, the Indians used snowshoes to travel through snow-covered fields and forests in winter. Today, some people in eastern Canada snowshoe for fun. Snowshoes look somewhat like tennis rackets. When people strap on these strange

123

Snowshoes were used by the Indians for walking over snow. Today snowshoeing is a popular spor[t]

shoes, they can travel over deep, soft snow quite rapidly, for their feet do not sink into the snow. Members of Canadian snowshoeing clubs wear colorful coats, sashes, and caps. Sometimes they have snowshoe races.

Baseball. If you were in Montreal* on a summer afternoon, you might watch the Montreal Royals play against an American baseball team. There are professional baseball teams in the cities of Toronto* and Vancouver,* as well as in Montreal. Also, men and boys throughout the country play in amateur* leagues. Thousands of people fill Canada's baseball parks each summer.

Golf and tennis. Many Canadian people enjoy playing golf and tennis in the summertime. Canada has some of the finest golf courses in the world. There are more than six hundred golf clubs throughout the country. Tennis is as popular as golf. Every year some of Canada's best amateur tennis players enter the Davis Cup* competition, an international tournament.

Playing golf. Some of the finest golf courses in the world are found in Canada.

A Canadian rodeo.* Every year in July there is an exciting rodeo in the city of Calgary.* Let us join the crowds of Canadians and visitors from the United States at the Calgary Stampede. First we visit an Indian village that is set up near the exhibition grounds. Then we take our seats in the crowded grandstand. In the arena, cowboys are riding bucking horses. These horses were brought in from the hills where they have been running wild. We watch other cowboys riding wild steers. Then there is a calf-roping contest. The most exciting event of all is the chuck-wagon race. The wagons almost tip over as they race wildly around a course shaped like a figure eight. The Calgary Stampede lasts a full week. People sometimes call it the "World Series" of all rodeos.

Canada's national parks. Today there are thirty-one national parks scattered throughout the provinces of Canada. Canadians

Riding a bull in the Calgary Stampede. This rodeo is held each July in the city of Calgary.*

Lake Louise is in Banff National Park.* There are thirty-one national parks in Canada.

are preserving these parks as natural playgrounds. People from other countries come to the parks for both winter and summer recreation. Canadian families enjoy the parks, too. They like to swim in the lakes and go picnicking and camping in the beautiful forests. Many visitors take pictures of the bears and the deer that roam through some of the parks.

DO YOU KNOW

1. Using pictures in this chapter, list the sports enjoyed by many Canadians.
2. Find a picture in this chapter of Canada's national sport.
3. Using the text and picture on page 126, describe the Calgary Stampede.
4. Tell of some of the things you could do in Canada's national parks.

Children from some Canadian farms travel by bus to large consolidated* schools.

CHAPTER THIRTEEN
EDUCATION

A visit to an elementary school. One school bus after another stops in front of a large elementary school in western Canada. Boys and girls wearing heavy overcoats and fur-lined boots hurry through the snow toward the front door. This is a consolidated* school, which serves eighteen rural school districts. It is a modern, two-story building made of brick and stucco. Many of the children who come here live on large wheat farms miles from the school.

As we enter a classroom, we see thirty children seated at desks arranged in neat rows. These children are in the fourth grade. The room is brightly lighted. The walls are painted a soft green. On the bulletin board at the back of the room we see some of the students' drawings. Many of them are pictures of animals and birds found in Canada.

We remain for a moment, listening to the teacher explain an arithmetic problem that is written on the blackboard at the front of the room. Later today, the children will have classes in English, social studies, and art.

If we visited a French-Canadian school in Quebec,* we would hear children and teachers in all classrooms speaking the French

Grade school children in Canada study arithmetic, social studies, and other subjects.

language. In this Canadian province about eight tenths of the people are French. Boys and girls from these French families speak French at home. They usually attend schools in which this language is spoken by everyone. Children in French schools learn to speak English as a second language when they are in the fifth grade.

In Canada, some children who live in the frozen northland, in dense forest regions, or on lonely plains cannot attend regular schools. Their families live so far away from villages that they cannot ride to school in buses. Schoolhouses on wheels are brought to these children. These are railroad cars that have been converted into schoolrooms and homes for the teachers. When a car and teacher arrive, children attend classes for several days.

A railroad car becomes a school on wheels for children who live far away from regular schools.

High school students may attend vocational* schools or schools that prepare them for college.

Then they are given homework to finish by the next time the school train visits them.

The children of many fishermen and loggers along the coast of British Columbia are picked up in a boat and taken to a central school each day. (See map on page 11.) In some places in the country there are one-room schools with only one teacher.

Canadian high schools. After completing the elementary grades, more than half of the students in Canada attend high school. Some students enroll in high school courses that prepare them for entrance into a college or university. They may study literature, languages, geography, history, mathematics, and science.

A vocational high school class. These boys learn carpentry, mechanics, and other skills.

Those boys and girls who plan to go to work after graduation take other courses. Sometimes they attend vocational* high schools. The boys learn to do skilled work such as carpentry, mechanics, or bookkeeping. Girls take business courses, or study sewing and cooking.

In the country, students attend large central high schools. Those who are planning to attend a university and those learning a trade study in the same building. Some of these schools provide dormitories for students who live too far from school to travel back and forth each day. Schools of this kind are also being built for the Indian children of the northern forests and the Eskimo children of the Arctic.

When French-Canadian boys in the province of Quebec finish the sixth grade, they enter either a vocational school, or a high school called a "classical college." Those who attend classical colleges study for eight years to enter a university.

French-Canadian girls in Quebec may enroll in special high schools when they finish the seventh grade. They may enter a school that teaches them cooking and sewing, or they may enter a school where they learn to be teachers or nurses. Some girls attend special high schools which prepare them for study at a university.

Higher education in Canada. There are many universities and colleges in Canada. Most provinces have at least one provincial university, somewhat like the state universities in the United States.

Students from remote areas can live in dormitories* in some of the country high schools.

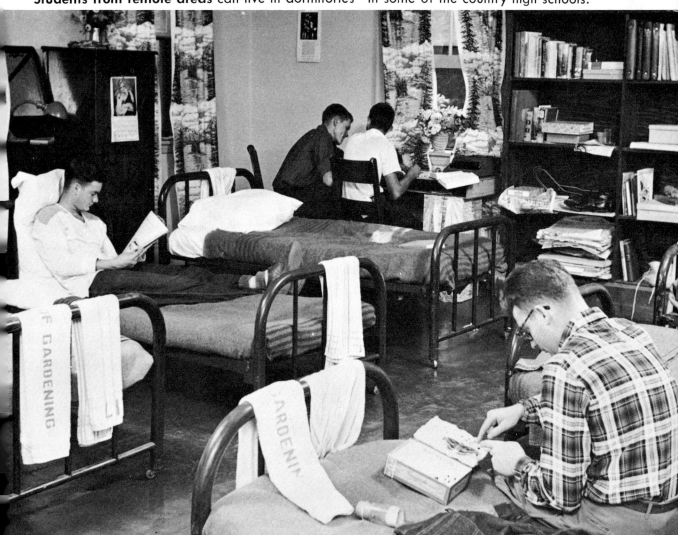

The University of Toronto is Canada's largest university. Laval University, in Quebec, is the oldest Canadian university. It began as a small Jesuit* school in 1635.

To enter a Canadian university or college, a student must have graduated from a high school or classical college. Usually, he must also pass a special entrance examination. At Canada's large universities, many students study to be doctors, dentists, lawyers, engineers, and scientists.

---DO YOU KNOW---

1. Name some of the subjects studied by Canadian children in elementary school.
2. Tell how teaching is provided for children who live far from village schools.
3. What do high school students study? What is a "classical college"?
4. Name two large universities in Canada. List the college entrance requirements.

A university class. Canada has several great universities and many smaller colleges.

A model Indian village. Indians and Eskimos lived in Canada long before Europeans came.

CHAPTER FOURTEEN
DISCOVERY AND SETTLEMENT

Early people of Canada. Tribes of Indians and Eskimos lived in Canada long before the white men came. In the forests along the Atlantic coast and the St. Lawrence River lived many tribes of Algonquin* Indians. The Iroquois* and Huron tribes lived near the Great Lakes. On Canada's Western Plains, the Blackfoot and Cree Indians hunted buffalo. Eskimos lived far to the north, along the shores of the Arctic Ocean.

Europeans come to Canada. About the year 1,000 A.D., Leif Ericson and some other Norsemen* sailed westward from the island of Greenland. On their voyage, they sighted a rocky shore line,

Leif Ericson and his crew of Norsemen were probably the first white men to see Canada.

which may have been the northeastern coast of Canada. These Norsemen were perhaps the first white men to see Canada.

The first European who is known to have landed in Canada was John Cabot. He and his son set sail from England in 1497. They were searching for a water route to the Orient.* After about a month at sea, they sighted the coast of Newfoundland.* A few miles off this coast, in shallow water, they found great shoals* of fish. There were so many they could dip them up in baskets. When Cabot returned to England, he told stories of these far-off seas filled with fish. His tales brought many adventurous fishermen from Europe to Canada's eastern shores.

The French explore and establish trading posts in Canada. Jacques Cartier* was the first European known to reach the interior of Canada. In 1534 he sailed along the coast of Newfoundland, searching for a passageway to China. Cartier sailed beyond Newfoundland and into the Gulf of St. Lawrence. (See map on page 11.) He landed on what is known today as the Gaspé Peninsula.* Cartier claimed this new land for France. The following year, Cartier made his second voyage to Canada. This time he traveled up the St. Lawrence to an Indian village at the site of the present city of Montreal.* Cartier traded for furs with friendly Indians. He realized that people in France would like to buy the beautiful furs of beavers and other animals. Later, fur trading became a profitable business for both the French and English.

Samuel de Champlain* founded the first permanent Canadian settlements. This great French explorer and trader is sometimes

John Cabot sailed from England to find a new route to the Orient.* He reached Canada instead.

called "The Father of Canada." In 1605, Champlain helped to found a little settlement at Port Royal, in what is now the province of Nova Scotia.* He had already explored the St. Lawrence, and in 1608 he established a trading post on the bank of this great river. The trading post grew to be the large city of Quebec.* In the years that followed, Champlain explored the territory of northern New York State and visited Lake Huron and Lake Ontario. He made friends with the Huron and Algonquin Indians.

Other French fur traders ventured far into the western wilderness. These men established several more trading posts along the St. Lawrence River. One of these posts became the city of Montreal. All the small French settlements were then united to form one colony called New France, with Quebec as the capital city.

Jacques Cartier* landed in Canada in 1534. The next year he explored the interior of Canada.

Samuel de Champlain,* a Frenchman, founded the first permanent white settlements in Canada.

The English trade for furs in Canada. English fur traders also began to trade with the Indians. Men of the Hudson's Bay Company* pushed west to the prairies and into the foothills of the Rocky Mountains. By the early 1700's many French and English trading posts dotted this territory.

War between the French and English. Both France and England wanted to control these lands in North America. For many years, each country had tried to become more powerful than the other

139

English troops defeated the French near the city of Quebec* in 1759.

on land and sea. Finally, the French built a chain of forts from New France to the city of New Orleans, which lay far to the south at the mouth of the Mississippi. Some of the French forts were built on land claimed by the English. The English sent a small group of soldiers to seize one of these forts in 1754. This was the beginning of the French and Indian War.*

In 1759, French and English armies fought a great battle near the city of Quebec. The English defeated the French and captured the city. A year later the English captured Montreal. In September, 1760, the French army surrendered to the English. By the

Treaty of Paris,* in 1763, Canada became a possession of Great Britain. England gained all the French possessions in Canada except two small islands off the coast of Newfoundland.

Many settlers come to Canada. In the years that followed, many people came from other countries to make their homes in Canada. During the American Revolution, thousands of American colonists who were loyal to the English king entered Canada. These people and many soldiers from the British army were given land in Canada.

During the first half of the nineteenth century, many settlers from the British Isles arrived in Canada. Among them were thousands of Irish families, who left their homeland to avoid starving

Scotsmen land at Nova Scotia.* After 1760, people from many countries came to live in Canada.

when the potato crops in Ireland failed. In the year 1847 alone, almost 100,000 people settled in this new land.

Canada wins responsible government. In 1791 the British government divided the region of Canada which is now occupied mainly by the provinces of Quebec* and Ontario* into two parts. The part that lay west of the Ottawa River was called "Upper Canada." The part that lay east of the river became "Lower Canada." There were mainly English and American colonists in the province of Upper Canada, and French colonists in the lower province. Each province was ruled by a governor sent from England. However, the people wanted a more democratic form of government. As time went on, colonists in both provinces became dissatisfied. Finally, in 1837, small riots broke out. Although these riots were

Early Canadian settlers worked hard to clear the land and build cabins in the wilderness.

Canadian leaders helped to unite several provinces into one nation, the Dominion of Canada.

stopped, the English government feared that the Canadians would revolt and fight for their independence. In 1840, the British government passed a law which united Upper and Lower Canada to form one province. The people of this province were allowed to elect an assembly of men to make their laws. Later, this more democratic form of government was also granted to the maritime provinces of Nova Scotia,* Prince Edward Island,* and New Brunswick.*

Canada becomes a dominion. On July 1, 1867, four Canadian provinces united to form one nation, called the Dominion of Canada. In years that followed, other Canadian provinces and two territories joined this union. Today, there are ten provinces and two territories within the Dominion.

Modern Canada. Although Canada has become a self-governing dominion, she remains a loyal member of the British Commonwealth of Nations.* In both world wars, Canadian men and women served alongside those of the United Kingdom, the United States, and other allied* countries. Canada is also a member of the United Nations. Her soldiers in the United Nations security forces* have served in many countries. At home, Canadians are working hard to develop their country's industrial and natural resources. They are helping promote peace and friendship among the nations of the world.

=== DO YOU KNOW ===

1. Tell of the adventures which brought white men to Canadian shores.
2. What French explorer and trader is known as "The Father of Canada"?
3. Explain how Canada became a possession of Great Britain
4. How many provinces and territories are there in Canada today?

Canadian soldiers served with the soldiers of Great Britain and her allies in two world wars.

Voting on election day. Canadians of voting age help choose the men who make Canada's laws.

CHAPTER FIFTEEN
GOVERNMENT

Canadians live in a democracy. The government of Canada is run by the people for the good of the people. Canadian men and women of voting age have the right to choose the people who make their country's laws. Every Canadian has the right to speak his opinion without fear. He may worship God in the church of his choice. He cannot be held in prison without a trial.

These and other rights and freedoms are based on old customs and court decisions. They are very carefully guarded by every

Queen Elizabeth II is the head of the Commonwealth of Nations.*
As a member of the Commonwealth, Canada shows
respect and loyalty to the Queen.

Canadian. They are so well understood that they are known as the unwritten part of Canada's Constitution. Every law made in Canada must agree with these principles of democratic government.

The responsibilities and duties of the Canadian government are recorded in the British North America Act and its amendments. This document was signed in 1867. In it are also recorded the powers of Canada's provincial governments.

The Governor General is the Queen's representative. Here, he inspects troops of an honor guard.

Canada belongs to the British Commonwealth of Nations. The Commonwealth of Nations is a group of independent nations and colonies with the Queen of England, Elizabeth II, at the head. As a member of the Commonwealth, Canada shows respect and loyalty to the Queen. However, like the other members of the Commonwealth, Canada has her own government and makes her own laws. Because she is an independent nation within the Commonwealth, and accepts the Queen as the head of the government, Canada is called a dominion.

The Dominion of Canada is a union of provinces. Canada is divided into ten provinces, which are united in much the same way as the

The Parliament Buildings. Parliament consists of the Governor General and two lawmaking bodies.

A meeting of the House of Commons. Canadians elect the members of this powerful governing body.

individual states of the United States. These provinces and Canada's two northern territories have their own governments. The central government of Canada is located in Ottawa.*

Parliament. The laws for the people of Canada are made by Parliament. The Canadian Parliament consists of the Governor General and two lawmaking houses. One of these is called the Senate, and the other, the House of Commons.

The Prime Minister* and Cabinet. These people do the real work of running the Canadian governm

The Governor General. The Governor General represents the Queen in Parliament and in the country. He is appointed by the Queen on the advice of the Canadian Prime Minister. The Governor General has many duties. He inspects troops, visits new industries, and officially welcomes heads of foreign governments,

150

just as the Queen might do if she were in Canada. He appoints men to positions in the government. He signs all new laws. However, because Canada is a self-governing country, the Governor General acts only at the request of the Canadian Prime Minister.

The House of Commons and the Senate. The 265 members of the House of Commons are elected by the Canadian people. These men serve for five years, unless an election is called at an earlier time.

The 102 members of the Senate are selected by the Prime Minister, and officially appointed by the Governor General. Members of the Senate hold their appointments for life.

Bills must be approved by both houses of Parliament and signed by the Governor General before they become laws. All money bills must be introduced in the House of Commons. This house is made up of representatives elected by the people. It is a more powerful governing body than the Senate.

The Prime Minister and his Cabinet direct the Canadian government. The real work of running the government is done by the Prime Minister and his Cabinet. The Prime Minister is the leader of the political party that has the most members in the House of Commons. He is chosen by his party and is appointed by the Governor General. The Prime Minister selects men from his party in Parliament to be Cabinet members. These men are then officially appointed by the Governor General. The Prime Minister and his Cabinet plan most of the important bills that are introduced in Parliament. Each Cabinet Minister is usually in charge of one government department.

The Prime Minister continues to act as the leader only so long as most of the members of the House of Commons support him and his Cabinet. If a majority in Parliament votes against him, he and his Cabinet must resign from office. However, at any time the Prime Minister can ask the Governor General to dismiss Parliament and call for a general election. Then the Canadian people may vote for new representatives in the House of Commons or re-elect the same members. However, such elections do not occur often in Canada. The Prime Minister can usually count on the support of Parliament.

Canada's courts protect the people's rights. The courts of Canada explain and uphold the laws, and protect the rights of the people. Each province has its own local courts which enforce the federal and provincial laws. The highest court in each province is the provincial supreme court.

The Exchequer Court* of Canada judges cases between Canadian citizens and the government of Canada. It decides questions concerning patents,* copyrights,* and shipping rights.

The highest court in Canada is the Supreme Court, which meets in Ottawa. This court consists of the Chief Justice and eight other judges. These judges, like all Canadian judges, are appointed by the federal government. People who feel they have not had a fair trial in a provincial supreme court or the Exchequer Court may take their cases to the Supreme Court. The judgment of this high court is final.

The governments of Canada's provinces. The government of each province is much like the central government in Ottawa. Each province has a Lieutenant Governor and an elected legislature, or lawmaking body. The leader of the political party having the most members in the legislature is called the Premier. The Premier and his Cabinet direct the provincial government. The Yukon Territory* and the Northwest Territories* are governed by commissioners. Each commissioner is assisted by a council. People in

Canada's cities, towns, villages, and counties govern themselves through elected councils.

─────────────────DO YOU KNOW─────────────────

1. In what ways is Canada's government like those of other democratic countries?
2. Explain why Canada is called a dominion. How does parliament make the laws?
3. Explain how Canada's courts protect the rights of the people.
4. Describe the government of Canada's provinces and territories.

The legislative chamber of one Canadian province. Each province has an elected lawmaking body.

GLOSSARY

Your study of Canada will be more interesting if you take time to use this glossary. You should turn to this glossary each time a word that you read in the text is marked with an asterisk (*), unless you clearly understand the word. The letters that appear inside the brackets following each word show you how the word should sound when it is correctly pronounced. The capital letters used in indicating the pronunciation show you which syllable of the word is to receive the chief stress, as: **Arvida** *(ahr VY duh)*.

The meaning of each word in the glossary is explained to help you understand the text and pictures in this book. You will learn much more about Canada if you will use this glossary.

Alberta *(al BUHR tuh)*. A province in western Canada, east of British Columbia. (See map, page 11.)

Algonquin *(al GAHNG kihn)* **Indians.** One of the largest and best-known groups of American Indians. Its members belong to many different tribes who are now living on reserves throughout eastern Canada.

allied *(uh LIDE)* **countries.** The groups of countries that fought against Germany in World War I or World War II.

amateur *(AM uh tuhr)* **leagues.** Associations of athletic teams. The players on these teams take part in sports for pleasure and not for money.

Annapolis Valley. The valley of the Annapolis River in western Nova Scotia. A well-known apple-growing region.

Arctic *(AHRK tihk)* **Circle.** An imaginary line around the earth, about 1,600 miles south of the North Pole. (See map, page 11.)

Arvida *(ahr VY duh)*. A city in south central Quebec. (See map, page 11.)

asbestos *(as BES tuhs)*. A grayish or greenish mineral fiber which will not burn. Used chiefly in making fireproof textiles and building materials.

aspen. A broad-leafed tree with small, thin leaves that tremble in the lightest breeze. The wood of the aspen is used chiefly for making paper pulp.

Baffin Island. An island northeast of Hudson Bay. It is the largest island in the Canadian Arctic Region. (See map, page 11.)

bands of Indians. Groups of Indians who live and work together. There are nearly six hundred separate Indian communities, known as "bands," in Canada.

Banff *(BAMF)* **National Park.** The oldest and second largest national park in Canada. Located on the eastern slope of the Rocky Mountains, in the province of Alberta.

Beauharnois *(boe ar NWA)* **plant.** A large hydroelectric plant located on the St. Lawrence River in southwestern Quebec. See **hydroelectric power.**

Bering *(BEER ihng)* **Strait.** A waterway that separates Asia from North America. It connects the Arctic Ocean and the Bering Sea. (See map, page 11.)

British Columbia. A mountainous province in western Canada. Bordered on the west by Alaska and the Pacific Ocean. (See map, page 11.)

British Commonwealth of Nations. A group of self-governing countries that accepts Queen Elizabeth II as its head. These nations are equal partners in the Commonwealth. This association helps each country, especially in matters of trade.

British Guiana *(ge AH nuh)*. A British colony on the northern coast of South America. One of the world's leading producers of aluminum ore.

Calgary *(KAL guh rih)*. One of the largest cities in western Canada. Located in southern Alberta Province, 80 miles east of the Canadian Rockies. (See map, page 11.)

caribou *(KARE ih boo)*. A kind of reindeer living in Greenland, Alaska, and Canada. Both male and female have antlers. Their coats are gray or light brown in summer and white in winter.

Cartier *(kar TYAY)*, **Jacques** *(ZHAK)*, 1491-1557. A French navigator and explorer who discovered the St. Lawrence River. (See picture, page 138.)

Caughnawaga *(kahg nuh WAHG uh)* **Reserve.** An Indian village in southern Quebec on the St. Lawrence River. Founded in 1667 as a refuge for Iroquois Indians converted to Christianity. See **Iroquois.**

Champlain *(sham PLAYN),* **Samuel de,** 1567?-1635. A famous French explorer.

Château Frontenac *(sha TOE frahn tuh NAK).* The largest hotel in the city of Quebec. See **Quebec.**

Coast Mountains. A mountain range extending about 1000 miles along the Pacific Coast of Canada and Alaska. (See map, page 11.)

combine *(KAHM bine).* A machine that cuts, threshes, and cleans grain while moving across a field.

Commonwealth of Nations. See **British Commonwealth of Nations.**

consolidated school. A central school, usually for both elementary and high school students from a number of rural school districts.

copyright. The sole right to reproduce, publish, and sell a literary or artistic work.

Davis Cup. A trophy given each year to the world champion tennis team. The cup has been won by either England, Australia, France, or the United States each year since it was donated in 1900.

diesel *(DEE zuhl)* **engines.** Engines that burn crude oil. Named after the German inventor Rudolf Diesel.

dormitories. Buildings in which students live while they are attending school away from home. Sleeping rooms.

drama festival. A series of plays or motion pictures presented during a special week, month, or season.

drought *(DROWT).* A long period of dry weather. Lack of rainfall.

Exchequer *(eks CHEK uhr)* **Court.** The court that decides all cases affecting the property and interests of the Canadian government.

foundries. Industrial plants where metals are melted and molded into particular shapes.

Fraser *(FRAY zuhr)* **River Valley.** The fertile valley of the Fraser River in the province of British Columbia.

French and Indian War (1755-1763). The last struggle between France and England for the possession of North America. See **Treaty of Paris.**

Gaspé *(GAS pay)* **Peninsula.** A peninsula in the province of Quebec. It extends along the south side of the St. Lawrence River and into the Gulf of St. Lawrence. (See map, page 90.)

geologists *(jee AHL o jihsts).* Scientists who study the earth's rocks and minerals.

Grand Banks. A shallow area in the Atlantic Ocean southeast of Newfoundland. One of the world's best fishing grounds. (See map, page 11.)

Group of Seven. Seven artists who traveled through Canada, painting scenes of their native land. The original members of the group were A. Y. Jackson, Lawren Harris, Arthur Lismer, James MacDonald, Frederick Varley, Franklin Carmichael, and Francis Johnston.

Gulf Stream. A warm ocean current from the Gulf of Mexico. Flows through the North Atlantic Ocean. (See map, page 25.)

hake. An important food fish, similar to the cod.

Halifax. Capital and largest city of the province of Nova Scotia, in southeastern Canada. Important fishing and shipbuilding center. Has one of the finest harbors in the world. (See map, page 11.)

Hudson's Bay Company. An organization formed in 1670 in England, for the purpose of trading with the Indians of British North America.

Huskies. Eskimo dogs of great strength, used for pulling sleds.

hydroelectric *(HY dro ee LEK trihk)* **power.** Electric power produced by the force of rushing water passing through turbines. See **turbines.**

Iroquois *(IHR o kwoi).* Indians included in a union of six tribes which originally inhabited New York State and southern Ontario. Today, the Iroquois live chiefly on reserves in Ontario and Quebec provinces.

Jackson, A. Y., 1882- . A Canadian artist who was an original member of the "Group of Seven." See **Group of Seven.**

Jamaica *(juh MAY kuh)*. A large British island in the Caribbean Sea. Located about 500 miles south of Florida.

Jesuit *(JEHZ yu iht)* **school.** A school established by the Society of Jesus, a Roman Catholic religious order.

Kane, Paul, 1810-1871. A Canadian artist noted for his paintings of Indian life and landscapes in western Canada.

kayak *(KY ak)*. An Eskimo canoe about 16 feet long, made of skins stretched over a wood or bone frame. The deck is completely covered except for a circular space in the center where the paddler sits. The paddler can lace himself in with an apron of skin to keep out the water.

Kicking Horse Pass. A mountain pass through the Canadian Rockies, located on the border between British Columbia and Alberta. (See map, page 11.)

Krieghoff *(KREEK hawf)*, **Cornelius,** 1812-1872. A wandering artist who began to paint in Canada about the middle of the 19th century.

Labrador *(LAB ruh dawr)*. A region that is part of the province of Newfoundland. Located northeast of Quebec Province, on the Atlantic Coast.

Labrador *(LAB ruh dawr)* **Current.** A cold ocean current that flows southward from Baffin Bay along the coast of Labrador and eastern Newfoundland. (See map, page 25.)

lichens *(LYE kuhnz)*. Very small, tough plants that can grow in almost any climate. They look like moss and are often seen on rocks and old stumps.

lock. A section of a canal that is used to raise or lower ships to different water levels. A gate at each end permits ships to enter or leave the lock. When a ship is in the lock, the gates are closed. The water level in the lock is raised or lowered to the level of the other part of the canal. Then the ship passes through the other gate.

long houses. Long, narrow, bark-covered homes once used by Iroquois Indians. One long house held from ten to twenty families.

Lord Strathcona *(strath KOE nuh)*. A Canadian government official who was active in the organization and success of the Canadian Pacific Railway.

marten *(MAHR ten)*. A valuable fur-bearing animal of the weasel family.

Montgomery, Lucy M., 1874-1942. Canadian novelist. Two of her best-known works are *Anne of Ingleside* and *Anne of Green Gables.*

Montreal *(mahn tree AWL)*. The largest city in Canada. Located in the province of Quebec, on an island in the St. Lawrence River. (See map, page 11.)

Morrice, James. 1865-1924. A Canadian painter whose work was admired by art critics in France. He lived much of his life in North Africa, France, and the West Indies.

natural gas. Gas often found in the earth near oil deposits.

New Brunswick. One of the ten provinces of Canada. It is bounded on the east by the Gulf of St. Lawrence, on the north by the province of Quebec, and on the west by the state of Maine. (See map, page 11.)

Newfoundland *(NYU fund land)* also *(nyu fund LAND)*. Canada's easternmost province. It is made up of the island of Newfoundland and its dependent territory on the mainland, Labrador. (See map, page 11.)

Norsemen. Daring bands of sea pirates who invaded the coasts of the British Isles and western Europe from about the 8th to the 10th centuries. They made many voyages throughout the North Atlantic. Some settled in Iceland and Greenland.

Northwest Territories. The vast area north of the Canadian provinces and east of the Yukon Territory. Consists of three districts: Mackenzie, Keewatin, and Franklin. (See map, page 11.)

Nova Scotia *(NOE vuh SKOE shuh)*. An eastern Canadian province made up of Cape Breton Island and a peninsula extending into the Atlantic Ocean. (See map, page 11.)

156

Okanagan *(oh kuh NAHG uhn)* **Valley.** The valley of the Okanagan River in southern British Columbia. This fertile region is well suited to farming, dairying, and fruitgrowing.

Ontario. *(ahn TAYR ih oe).* One of the ten provinces of Canada. It is bordered on the south by the Great Lakes, and on the north by Hudson Bay. (See map, page 11.)

Orient. The East. Countries east of the Mediterranean Sea. Often used to mean the countries of Asia.

Ottawa *(AHT uh wuh).* The capital city of Canada. Located in southeast Ontario, on the Ottawa River. See **Ontario.**

parka. A long, shirtlike garment with a hood that can be pulled over the head.

patent. An official paper issued by the government, giving an inventor control of the manufacture and sale of his invention for a certain number of years.

Peace Tower. A beautiful tower, almost three hundred feet high. It is an important feature of Canada's main Parliament Building. This tower is a memorial to the Canadian soldiers who gave their lives in World War I. (See picture, page 148.)

petroleum. *(pee TROE lee um).* Crude mineral oil as it is found in the ground. Used to make gasoline and many other products.

pollack *(PAHL uhk).* A dark-colored North Atlantic food fish belonging to the cod family.

Prime Minister. The responsible head of the Canadian government. Leader of the executive branch of government.

Prince Edward Island. The smallest of Canada's ten provinces. Located in the Gulf of St. Lawrence off the coasts of Nova Scotia and New Brunswick. (See map, page 11.)

Quebec *(kwee BEHK).* The capital city of Quebec Province. Located on the north bank of the St. Lawrence River, in southeast Canada. (See map, page 11.)

Quebec *(kwee BEHK)* **Province.** The oldest and largest province in Canada. Located in eastern Canada between Hudson Bay and the Gulf of St. Lawrence. (See map, page 11.)

reserves. Land set aside by the government for the special use of Indians. Similar to Indian reservations in the United States.

reservoir *(REZ uhr vwahr).* A place where a large amount of water is stored for later use.

Rideau *(ree DOE)* **Canal.** A water route over a hundred miles long, which consists of the Rideau River, several lakes and some short canals. It connects the Ottawa River with Lake Ontario.

rodeo *(ROE dee oe).* Public entertainment presenting the features of a Western roundup, such as lariat throwing, riding bucking horses, and roping cattle.

St. John Valley. The fertile valley of the St. John River in the province of New Brunswick.

St. Lawrence Seaway. A great water highway. It extends from the Atlantic Ocean up the St. Lawrence River and through the Great Lakes. (See map, page 90.)

Sault Ste. Marie *(SOO saynt muh REE).* A city in southern Ontario. Located on the St. Marys River, which flows between Lake Huron and Lake Superior. (See map, page 90.)

Scandinavia *(skan duh NAY vih uh).* The name given to an area in northern Europe which includes the countries of Norway, Sweden, and Denmark.

schooners. Sailing vessels with two or more masts and fore and aft sails. They are economical to operate, because few men are needed to handle the sails.

Service, Robert, 1874-1958. A Canadian poet and novelist. He wrote poems and stories of the rough life of miners, hunters and trappers in frontier days.

Shakespeare *(SHAYK speer),* **William,** 1564-1616. Considered the greatest writer of plays ever known, and the finest poet in English literature.

shoals *(SHOLZ)* **of fish.** A great number of fish swimming together. Also called "schools" of fish.

sluice *(SLOOS).* A long trough for washing gold-bearing earth. Dirt and gravel are washed away by water, while the gold remains in the sluice.

smelters. Ovens in which metal ore is melted to separate the metal from the waste material.

soapstone. A soft stone which feels soapy or oily to the touch.

Southampton Island. A large island located at the northwest entrance of Hudson Bay. (See map, page 11.)

spirits. To the early Eskimos, spirits were like unseen powers which lived in people, animals, or even in objects such as sticks or stones. They believed these "spirits" were responsible for the good or evil things in their lives.

Steep Rock. A lake in western Ontario near the United States border. This lake and the surrounding area is rich in valuable iron ore deposits.

Stratford *(STRAT fuhrd).* A city located in southeastern Ontario, west of Toronto. (See map, page 11.)

stucco. A cementlike material often used to form a hard covering for outside wall surfaces.

tap. To bore a hole in the trunk of a sugar-maple tree to obtain the sap. A small spout is placed in the hole and a bucket is hung from the spout.

tobacco curing. A drying process to prepare tobacco for market.

topping. Cutting the top off a tall tree, before the tree itself is felled.

Toronto *(tuh RAHN toe).* Capital city of the province of Ontario. Located at the west end of Lake Ontario. (See map, page 11.)

totem *(TOE tuhm)* **poles.** Wooden poles, made from cedar trees. The Indians carve figures of men, animals, birds, and fish, one above the other, into the tree trunks. The figures tell stories of past events and Indian heroes. (See picture, page 111.)

trawler. A fishing boat used to drag large nets along the ocean bottom.

Treaty of Paris. A treaty of peace, signed at Paris in 1763, officially ending the French and Indian war. See **French and Indian War.**

tullibee *(TUHL ih bee).* A food fish found in Lake Winnipeg and nearby waters, and in the north central United States. Related to the whitefish.

tundras *(TOON druhs).* The treeless and often marshy plains of the arctic regions. The ground remains frozen all year, except for the few inches of topsoil which thaw in the summer.

turbines *(TUHR bihnz).* Engines run by the force of rushing water striking against blades fitted on a driveshaft. Used to drive electric generators.

Ukraine *(yu KRAYN).* An important agricultural region in the Soviet Union, bordering the Black Sea.

Ukrainian. Refers to the Ukraine, its language, or its people. See **Ukraine.**

Union of Soviet Socialist Republics. Also Soviet Union, U.S.S.R., or Russia. Made up of fifteen republics located in Europe and Asia.

United Nations security forces. Troops from many countries, sent by the United Nations organization to certain troubled areas of the world. There they try to preserve peace and order.

U.S.S.R. See **Union of Soviet Socialist Republics.**

Vancouver *(van KOO vuhr).* The third largest city in Canada and the chief Canadian seaport on the Pacific. Located in southwest British Columbia. (See map, page 11.)

Victoria. The capital city of the province of British Columbia. Located at the southeastern end of Vancouver Island. (See map, page 11.)

vocational high schools. High schools that train students in skills needed for certain occupations.

Williams, Ralph Vaughan, 1872-1958. An English composer. Best known for his *London Symphony* and *Sea Symphony.*

Winnipeg. The capital city of Manitoba. Located in the south central part of this province. The city was named for Lake Winnipeg, forty-five miles to the north. (See map, page 11.)

Winnipeg Music Festival. A series of musical concerts held each year at Winnipeg, in the province of Manitoba.

Yukon *(YOU kahn)* **Territory.** The large, mountainous region in the northwestern part of Canada. Whitehorse is the capital city. (See map, page 11.)

Index

(Page numbers in this Index that are preceded by "*p.*" refer to pictures.)